the complete guide to

buying and renting your

first home

3RD EDITION

niki chesworth

KOGAN
PAGE

Publisher's note
Every possible effort has been made to ensure that the information contained in this book is accurate at the time of going to press, and the publishers and authors cannot accept responsibility for any errors or omissions, however caused. No responsibility for loss or damage occasioned to any person acting, or refraining from action, as a result of the material in this publication can be accepted by the editor, the publisher or any of the authors.

First published in Great Britain in 1998 as *A Practical Guide to Buying and Renting Your First Home*
Second edition 1999
Third edition 2004 as *The Complete Guide to Buying and Renting Your First Home*

Kogan Page Limited
120 Pentonville Road
London N1 9JN
United Kingdom
www.kogan-page.co.uk

© Niki Chesworth, 1998, 1999, 2004

British Library Cataloguing in Publication Data

A CIP record for this book is available from the British Library.

ISBN 0 7494 4157 7

Typeset by Saxon Graphics Ltd, Derby
Printed and bound in Great Britain by Biddles Limited, King's Lynn, Norfolk

Contents

Contents

1 Introduction

Ten or twenty years ago, you would probably have expected to own your first home after a brief period of renting or flat sharing.

In the mid-1980s, that is exactly what I did. The flats I shared and rented when I was at college and in my first job were never really 'home'. At 23 I bought a three-bedroom recently renovated house in London – my first real home. If I was that age today, I doubt I would be able to afford to buy even a pokey little flat in a place nobody wanted to live.

Incomes have simply not kept pace with house price inflation and affordability is now the biggest problem facing first-time buyers. This is why this book looks at renting as well as buying your first home. It also covers alternative ways to get onto the property ladder, from buying with your parents to shared ownership and affordable housing schemes.

The average price paid by first-time buyers has increased by 294 per cent over the past 20 years with the average UK property now costing five times the average earnings of a full-time male employee.

No wonder first-time buyers are becoming extinct.

The number of first-time buyers is now at its lowest level since records began in 1974. Only 174,000 first-time buyers entered the property market in the first six months of 2003, compared to 253,000 in the first six months of 2002.

To afford to get onto the property ladder first-time buyers now have to put down an average of almost £20,000 as a deposit on the average-priced first-time buyer home of £103,294 (which costs 128 per cent more than 10 years ago). It takes them years to save up. No wonder the average first-time buyer is now aged 33.

However, historically low interest rates mean that, for the majority of first-time buyers affordability remains very good despite the high price to earnings ratios, particularly in the south. The average first-time buyer in the UK is spending just 16.5 per cent of average gross earnings on mortgage payments, compared with 18 per cent in 1993 and 22.8 per cent five years ago.

This research has been based on a combination of data from the Halifax, the Council of Mortgage Lenders Survey of Mortgage Lenders and Office of National Statistics figures.

Prices shown in the tables are arithmetic average prices of houses – otherwise known as crude averages – on which an offer of mortgages has been granted. These prices are not standardized and therefore can be affected by changes in the sample from quarter to quarter – as such, care should be taken when comparing prices. Figures exclude properties sold for £1 million plus.

Table 0.1   FTB average house price – regional

Region	FTB Average House Price £				
	1993	1998	2003 *	% Change 5 years ago	% Change 10 years ago
North	35,456	39,131	60,605	55	71
Yorks & The Humber	38,169	42,061	66,755	59	75
N.West	40,511	45,847	70,590	54	74
E.Mids	38,348	44,784	86,691	94	126
W.Mids	42,824	49,814	90,747	82	112
E.Ang	42,554	53,033	109,557	107	157
S.West	43,483	54,967	116,795	112	169
S.East	51,735	69,083	142,577	106	176
Gr.Lon	63,881	96,923	193,508	100	203
Wales	37,873	43,659	68,834	58	82
Scot	40,918	46,909	63,389	35	55
N.Ire	31,111	49,473	74,880	51	141
UK	45,249	56,490	103,294	83	128

* period July 2002 – June 2003
Source: Halifax

Table 0.2 FTB average deposit – regional

Region	1993	1998	FTB Deposit 2003 *	% Change 5 years ago	% Change 10 years ago
North	3,477	4,601	8,140	77	134
Yorks & The Humber	4,114	5,160	10,160	97	147
N.West	4,425	5,682	10,307	81	133
E.Mids	4,362	5,803	15,013	159	244
W.Mids	4,985	7,138	16,433	130	230
E.Ang	5,235	7,734	21,616	179	313
S.West	4,958	8,304	23,123	178	366
S.East	6,169	10,855	29,669	173	381
Gr.Lon	9,319	18,600	40,095	116	330
Wales	3,890	5,643	10,139	80	161
Scot	5,259	6,131	9,162	49	74
N.Ire	3,559	7,138	10,244	44	188
UK	5,433	8,502	18,950	123	249

* period July 2002 – June 2003
Source: Halifax

Table 0.3 FTB average deposit as % of earnings

Region	FTB Average Deposit % Earnings 1993	1998	2003 *
North	21	23	34
Yorks & The Humber	25	26	42
N.West	25	27	40
E.Mids	26	29	62
W.Mids	30	34	65
E.Ang	31	38	85
S.West	29	41	97
S.East	29	41	120
Gr.Lon	39	63	140
Wales	24	29	30
Scot	30	30	38
N.Ire	24	41	N/a
UK	30	38	72

* period July 2002 – June 2003
Source: Halifax House Price Index, earnings data from ONS

Table 0.4   Average age of FTB

Region	1993	1998	2002
N. Ire	34	32	32
Scot	38	34	35
Wales	31	32	33
N. West	30	31	32
W. Mids	30	31	33
S. West	32	32	34
S. East	32	32	33
Gr. Lon	32	31	32
E. Ang	32	32	34
E. Mids	31	31	32
Yorks & The Humber	31	31	33
North	32	32	33
UK	32	32	33

Source: CML

Table 0.5   House price: earnings ratio

Region	1993	1998	2003 *
North	2.12	1.99	2.55
Yorks & The Humber	2.32	2.14	2.74
N.West	2.33	2.16	2.77
E.Mids	2.32	2.22	3.59
W.Mids	2.54	2.39	3.60
E.Ang	2.51	2.61	4.33
Wales	2.36	2.23	2.90
S.West	2.51	2.69	4.71
S.East	2.42	2.64	4.98
Gr.Lon	2.66	3.30	5.75
Scot	2.36	2.29	2.64
UK	2.46	2.54	3.92

* period July 2002 – June 2003
Source: Halifax. Earnings figures based on income of main earner
This research has been based on a combination of data from the Halifax, the Council of
Mortgage Lenders Survey of Mortgage Lenders and Office of National Statistics figures.

The property market

The recent small increase in interest rates from their 30-year low, fears that capital gains tax may be levied on the profits made when you sell your home as well as recent increases in stamp duty on the purchase of property have led pundits to predict that recent rampant house price inflation simply cannot last.

Any slow-down in house price inflation can only be good news for first-time buyers. However, do not bank on a dramatic fall in property values.

When the last edition of this book was published in 1999 the experts were also predicting a property crash following rampant house price inflation, which saw prices rise by around 40 per cent since their trough in 1995. This crash never happened. Why? Interest rates remained low, which meant that mortgages were more affordable. Unemployment was falling and it was never easier to borrow so much.

The same applies today. Even if the number of jobless and the cost of borrowing increases, these are still near their historical lows.

The following are key drivers of the housing market. When the cost of borrowing and/or unemployment rises, increasing numbers of borrowers struggle to make their monthly mortgage repayments, with some forced to sell. This can lead to a sudden glut of properties for sale by desperate homeowners and in turn that leads to a fall in prices. However, employment levels are still historically high, and borrowing costs historically low.

Supply and demand: The need for millions of new homes in the South East, a rising number of households and the desire for home ownership, mean there is also a lack of supply to meet growing demand.

If the current low level of new house-building continues, there will be a major shortage of homes in the United Kingdom by the year 2020, according to Britain's biggest mortgage lender, the Halifax. The rise in the number of single-person households is fuelling the demand. However, while the average household is getting smaller, three- and four-bedroomed detached properties are still the most common type being built.

New house-building peaked at over 414,000 in 1968. In 2002 only 170,000 new homes were built in Britain, slightly above the 2001 figure, which was the lowest total of new homes built in any year since 1947.

This in itself will keep property values high so it looks like the property market will still be a good investment – even if there is the occasional 'blip'.

Low interest rates: The low cost of borrowing is also fuelling house price inflation. The average borrower is spending around 14 per cent of average gross earnings on mortgage interest payments – well below the long-run average of 21 per cent, according to the Halifax.

So, although mortgage interest rates have increased from their lowest levels since the mid-1960s, as around half of all new borrowers before the recent base rate rises were electing to take a fixed-rate mortgage, any bank base rate rises will have less of an impact.

Even if existing borrowers are hit by base rate rises, these are likely to cause little pain as many of these have much smaller mortgages. A 0.25 per cent rise in base rates costs a borrower with an £80,000 mortgage just £4 a week.

Affordability: The average loan to value is currently 66 per cent – down slightly from 67 per cent in 2002 but well down from the figures in 1993 when this rose to 78 per cent, according to the Council of Mortgage Lenders. This increase in equity – as a result of house price rises – will cushion the impact of any downturn in the property market. It also means there is far less of a risk of negative equity – the problem of the last house price crash in the late 1980s and early 1990s when homebuyers were left with mortgage debts larger than the value of their property.

So while house price inflation is slowing, prices are still rising well above inflation.

However, it is not just investing that appeals to homebuyers. Nesting also matters. There is nothing like the feeling of owning your own home.

Renting v buying

In earlier editions of this book, we looked at the pros and cons of renting versus buying, to help readers with their choice. However, today, few first-timers have a choice. Renting generally has to come first because few can afford to buy their first home. In fact, the average age of a first-time buyer is now 33 – so many will have rented several properties before taking their first step onto the property ladder.

The number of first-time buyers coming onto the market is at its lowest level since records began in 1974 with the number of first-time buyers in the first six months of 2003 32 per cent lower than in the same period of 2002.

Few have the luxury of choice. The average first-time buyer puts down a deposit of almost £20,000 – a substantial amount particularly as many will already have had to deal with student debts of around £10,000.

The increase in the supply of good quality rented accommodation thanks to the introduction of buy-to-let mortgages, means that those who cannot afford to buy can still find a decent home.

You can tell how popular private rented accommodation has become by the number of estate agents that now offer as many – or more – properties for rent as they do for sale.

However, the number of those renting is still a fraction of the number of people buying their own home.

The UK has one of the highest levels of homeownership in the world with 7 in 10 homes owner-occupied – only 1 in 10 is rented from a private landlord.

The cost comparison

Although renting is seen as an easy and affordable alternative to buying, it can be as expensive – if not more so. Private landlords buy with the aim of renting out a property for more than the cost of borrowing to buy the property, so rents are rarely much cheaper than mortgage costs. The main advantage of renting is that you do not need a deposit and do not have the expense of long-term maintenance, insuring the property, furnishing it or decorating it – and there is no financial risk involved. Renters do not have to bear the brunt of sharp increases in interest rates or worry that the price may fall.

But while there is no risk in renting, there is also no reward. As the saying goes 'Rent money is dead money'. Those who buy will, after 25 years or so, own their property outright and will – if past trends continue – see substantial capital appreciation. Those who rent will have to keep paying rent forever and will never have the freedom of owning a substantial asset.

Table 0.6   Average saving of buying v renting in the UK over 25 years

Type of House	Total cost of renting	Total cost of buying	Saving	% Saving from buying v renting
Two-bedroom flat	£277,819	£185,557	£92,262	33%
Three-bedroom terraced	£302,890	£213,042	£89,848	29%
Three-bedroom semi-detached	£314,884	£238,338	£76,546	24%
Four-bedroom detached	£492,238	£429,884	£62,354	13%

Source: Abbey National

Over the longer term – 25 years – it is on average 24 per cent or around £80,250 cheaper to buy than rent a home in the United Kingdom, according to the Abbey National.

The gap has narrowed from 30 per cent more expensive in 2002 as a result of rising property prices.

As a result, over the longer term you are likely to pay more in rent than you would in mortgage repayments. While your mortgage repayments may seem high initially, over the long run your salary will usually increase and inflation will reduce the cost of repayments in real terms. So after 5 or 10 years your mortgage payments will take up a smaller proportion of your income. Rents, on the other hand, rise and as a result will generally take up the same proportion of your income.

Who should rent?

Although most people want to buy their own home, for some it is not practical or advisable. These include:

- Those who cannot afford to get onto the property ladder (either because their salary is not large enough or they do not have a lump sum to cover the costs/deposit).

- Those who want to buy, but would rather save up a deposit first (those with larger deposits generally qualify for cheaper mortgages).

- Those who have uncertain income and cannot commit to regular mortgage payments.

- Those who do not have a permanent job but are on a fixed contract (these people can find it harder to qualify for a mortgage and, if they do, the mortgage rate may be higher).

- Those who expect to move home in the near future or want the flexibility to move towns/cities for employment purposes.

■ Those who do not yet want the responsibility of owning a property (for instance they are working too hard to want to spend time decorating and furnishing a home).

■ Those who fear they may lose their job in the near future. If you are unemployed your rent will usually be paid for you by Social Security provided it is a reasonable rent for the area you are living in and you are over 25. If you buy a home you may not receive any help from Social Security to meet your mortgage interest payments for the first nine months. So unless you have mortgage protection insurance – and even if you have insurance it may not pay out if you claim shortly after taking out the policy – you may risk losing your home.

Who should buy?

■ Those with a regular income who will – if they take out the best value mortgage – often find they can buy more cheaply than they can rent.

■ Those who are established in an area and expect to live and work there for the next few years.

■ Those who are prepared to take on the responsibility of homeownership – maintenance, repairs, a commitment to meet monthly mortgage payments, etc.

■ Those wanting the freedom of homeownership – being able to decorate their home as they wish and not having a landlord breathing down their necks.

■ Those wanting to cut their housing costs – for instance by renting out rooms so that their monthly mortgage bills are far lower than the rent on a similar property.

Pros and cons of renting

Pros:
You do not need a large deposit.

Flexibility to move.

No responsibility for maintenance/repairs/ redecoration.

Pros:
You can often rent a nicer property than you could afford to buy because lenders restrict the amount you can borrow, whereas landlords only want to know that you can afford the rent.

If you run into financial difficulties you can easily move to cheaper accommodation.

Cons:
No capital appreciation.

It is not *your* home.

You may have to move after six months/a year, particularly if the property is let on a shorthold tenancy.

Cons:
When you renew your tenancy or rents are reviewed, your rent may increase or the property may no longer be affordable.

If you delay buying you may find that prices have increased so much you can no longer afford to buy.

Pros and cons of buying

Pros:
It is *your* home, you can decorate it as you wish and do not have the problem of dealing with a landlord.

You, not a landlord, can decide when you want to move.

Cons:
It is a major responsibility and a financial drain as you have to pay for maintenance/ repairs

If mortgage rates rise and house prices fall you may not be able to pay your mortgage/

Once you have repaid your mortgage you will no longer have to pay to live in the property (unlike renters) and should own a substantial asset.

Mortgage repayments can be cheaper than rent and if you get into financial difficulties you can rent out a room to help pay the mortgage.

may be unable to sell as your mortgage debt is greater than the value of the property.

If you cannot pay your mortgage your home may be repossessed and you will find it difficult to obtain mortgage finance in the future.

Homebuying and renting – the future

As this book goes to press there are a number of unknowns.

A new Housing Act is expected to come into force in the next few years. This will change the way houses are bought, thanks to the introduction of the Home Information Packs (widely known as seller's packs) and improving the lot for those who rent properties. However, while the Housing Bill has been published there may be further changes as it passes through parliament. It should herald greater help for first-time buyers with a boost in affordable housing.

The new Commonhold and Leasehold Reform Act 2002 is also still coming into force – the introduction of commonhold is expected in 2004. There are also fears that there will be further increases in stamp duty and possibly the introduction of capital gains tax on the profits made on the sale of your main home. Currently all gains are usually tax-free.

Readers are advised to keep abreast of these changes, particularly as they could affect their choices. A new Key Worker Housing Initiative, for example, could mean help in getting onto the property ladder for those in certain professions.

Part 1
Renting

1 What is available and affordable?

Nearly a third of the population rents their homes with 1 in 10 renting from private landlords. So the private rented sector plays an important part in the housing market providing an additional housing choice for those who cannot or are not yet ready to buy their own homes.

With the average age of first-time buyers rising to 33 (as getting onto the property ladder becomes less affordable), renting is often the only choice when it comes to your first home.

Most privately rented properties are owned by small investors, often with only one or two properties in their portfolio, rather than large landlords. These properties are increasingly bought as buy-to-let investments and the quality of the accommodation is usually quite high – to maximize the rental yield.

To protect both the landlord and the tenant, most renters should find that they are covered by written tenancy agreements, usually under the assured shorthold tenancies.

Most of the problems that arise are usually as a result of a misunderstanding about what was agreed at the outset.

What type of accommodation?

Your choice will depend largely on how much you can afford. The options are:

▌ renting a room/becoming a lodger;

- sharing a rented flat or house with friends;

- taking out a tenancy/lease on a flat or house.

Furnished or unfurnished?

The decision will generally depend on whether or not you have a substantial amount of furniture. If you don't have many belongings a furnished property is likely to be the cheapest and easiest option.

The demand for unfurnished accommodation has increased in recent years, but most of this has come from families who intend to rent for a long period and want to establish their own home. As a result the rents on unfurnished properties tend to be higher reflecting the better quality of this type of accommodation.

At the same time new fire regulations have made it preferable for landlords to rent unfurnished properties as they can no longer furnish homes with second-hand furniture or old cast-offs. Another factor influencing the increased availability of unfurnished accommodation is that landlords now have more protection against sitting tenants. In the past landlords were advised to furnish property to avoid this risk, but now there is no legal distinction between furnished and unfurnished accommodation.

Stamp duty

Under the Stamp Duty Act, technically tenants have to pay 1 per cent of the annual rent (or part thereof if the property is let for less than a year) if the property is unfurnished. Furnished property carries a stamp duty of just £1 provided the tenancy is for less than a year. Furnished lettings for longer than 12 months attract stamp duty at 1 per cent. However, in practice this rarely happens and even if the tenancy agreement is unstamped the contract is still valid.

Finding somewhere to rent

Friends and family

This is usually the easiest way to find a room to rent. However, make sure you have an agreement to protect yourself should you fall out and then be asked to leave with little or no notice. To save arguments at a later date, agree (preferably in writing) what you do and do not have to pay for.

Becoming a lodger

The days when renting a room in a house or flat was a bit like joining the cast of *Rising Damp* are long over. The government's Rent-A-Room scheme, which allows homeowners to rent out one room in their home tax free provided the rent is not more than £4,250 in a tax year, means that an increasing number of rooms are being rented out. The advantage is that the owner can only rent out one room under this scheme so you will not be living in a house full of bedsits. Also, because the owner must live in the property it will generally be furnished to a good standard and be well maintained.

Flat share services

These tend to be targeted at young people, so the advantage is that you are likely to be sharing with people of a similar age. However, remember you may be living in close proximity to strangers and this can cause problems, particularly if one sharer is particularly noisy, fails to pay his or her rent on time, leaves a mess or makes a habit of eating your food. If the other sharers want to move out you could be left with the responsibility for paying the entire rent or for advertising for new flatmates. If you cannot find new sharers or afford the rent, you may be forced to move out.

The advantages of sharing with someone who owns the property are that they will take responsibility for maintenance and repairs and will be more approachable than some faceless landlord. However, if the owner lives in the property he or she is likely to be more fussy about cleanliness and noise and you may feel it is their home, not yours.

Newspaper/magazine advertisements

These often offer relatively cheap accommodation (unless the advertisement is placed by a letting agent). Make sure you have a formal tenancy agreement to protect you from rogue landlords. Renting directly from the landlord will often mean that you will have a more personal relationship. This can be a disadvantage or an advantage depending on the personalities involved.

The jargon

When looking through classified advertising it may be difficult to decipher the terminology:

apt	apartment	gdn	garden
c/h	central heating	hs	house
dbl,db	double	lge	large
ff	fully furnished	n/s	non-smoker
f/ft	fully fitted	pkg	parking
fl,flt	flat	prof	professional
gge	garage	sgl	single
sh	shared, as in sh kit and bath (shared kitchen and bathroom)	shwr	shower
		spac	spacious

Housing associations

This accommodation is usually restricted to those who meet the criteria of the association – which often means you have to be homeless or spend months or even years on a waiting list.

However, you may be able to part-rent and part-buy under the Shared Ownership Scheme without having a long wait, particularly if you are an 'essential' worker – a nurse or teacher, for example. See Chapter 5: From renter to buyer.

Warning: Be careful when responding to newspaper advertisements. If you are a single woman take a friend along when you view the property. Do not part with any money on the spot, however desperate you are to rent the property. It has been known for crooks to show tenants round flats and then demand the deposit and first month's rent in cash, only to disappear before the tenant realizes that the bogus landlord does not own the property.

Developers/property companies

Some property developers and other residential investment companies are now building new homes for rent rather than sale. The advantages of these are that the properties are brand new or only a few years old and as such should be in good condition.

Letting agents

You will be required to pay an administration fee. In return you should find that the landlord is reputable, your deposit is protected as it is held in a bank account controlled by the letting agent and the agent will have a legally prepared tenancy agreement. If you are using a reputable company (for instance, a member of the Association of Residential Letting Agents) you should not have to pay introductory fees or fees for being listed on the agent's books, but you will have to pay for inventories, administration, preparation of the tenancy agreement and for the agent to take up references.

Many established firms are members of the Association of Residential Lettings Agents (01494 431 680). Visit its Web site, www.arla.co.uk, and look up *Information for Tenants* – a question and answer section covering the questions every tenant should ask. Alternatively, request *Trouble Free Letting – what every landlord and tenant should ask.*

Other professional organizations of which reputable letting agents may be members include the National Association of Estate Agents, the Royal Institution of Chartered Surveyors and the National Approved Letting Scheme. All of these agents are subject to standards of service and hold your money in separate bank accounts protected by insurance to cover against negligence and theft, fraud or misappropriation.

Always use a reputable agent – despite the risks, some tenants still use unregulated letting agents. It is not unknown for these agents to disappear or to go into liquidation taking rent and deposits with them.

Warning: Letting agents should not charge you just for registering on their books. However, some do charge a 'holding deposit' from tenants, which is paid once a suitable property is found. This charge can range from £50 to £200. If you have to pull out of the tenancy the deposit will usually be kept by the agent. A few do not return this holding deposit even if the tenancy goes ahead. So always check what charges will be made, get a signed receipt and ask for any terms and conditions to be put in writing.

Budgeting for the costs

Although the initial costs involved in renting are far lower than buying, you will often still require a lump sum of at least £1,000.

The deposit

You will usually be required to pay a deposit of between one month and six weeks' rent. This deposit covers the landlord against damage to the property or fixtures and fittings as well as the cost of returning the property to the state in which it was rented to you.

Rent in advance

In addition to the deposit, you will also be required to pay a month's rent in advance. Landlords often require standing orders for payment of the rent to ensure that it is paid on time. If you don't pay by standing order or direct debit make sure you have a rent/receipt book.

Also note that some tenancy agreements give the landlord the right to charge interest on late payment of rent.

Agent's fees

If you are using a letting agent the administration fees should have been agreed in advance. Fees are often in the region of £100 to £150. Remember, VAT is added to fees. If you have taken out a tenancy for only a short period of time (for instance, six months) and then want to renew the agreement you will then have to pay a second lot of fees to extend the tenancy (although these should not be as high as the fees to cover the initial agreement).

Holding deposits (usually a nominal amount) can be required when you make an offer on a property. If, for any reason, you decide not to go ahead by an agreed date, the holding deposit or part of it will be retained against administrative costs already incurred by the letting agent.

Otherwise it will usually be offset against the first rent and full deposit payments. If the landlord decides not to proceed then the holding deposit will be returned. Paying a holding deposit in no way legally obliges either party to enter into the tenancy.

Do not confuse a holding deposit with a fee charged by agents simply for registering on their books.

Costs after you have moved in

You should not forget to budget for additional costs once you have moved in. Some of these – such as insurance – may have to be paid as soon as you move and at a time when you may be struggling financially after paying for the deposit and a month's rent in advance.

- You will generally have to pay your own council tax as this will not be included in the rent.

- It will usually be your responsibility to obtain a TV licence – even if the landlord provides a television in the property – unless you are a lodger.

- Gas and electricity bills (although the landlord normally pays the water rates).

- You will be responsible for telephone bills – and any connection fees.

- You need to take out insurance for your own contents/possessions.

Viewing a property

When you purchase a home you view the property several times, arrange a survey and make detailed checks from whether the central heating works to whether there is any damp. But most of those renting a flat usually make their decision after only a brief five-minute inspection.

Remember you are making a commitment to rent for a certain period of time (notice in the first few months is often 12 weeks) so if, after moving in, you find the property is not suitable you will be forced to live there for several months.

The reason why it is essential to inspect the property carefully is that you are agreeing to take on that property 'as seen'. Landlords do not have to change or alter the property, fixtures or furnishings once the tenancy has started. They only have to repair or replace items that are broken or no longer work properly. So if the central heating is inadequate in the depths of winter, you will have to tolerate the cold. The landlord does not have to install additional radiators and is only responsible for ensuring the central heating works properly and is safe.

Remember, letting agents represent the landlord, not the tenant, even though you are paying them a fee. So the agent is unlikely to tell you that the flat is draughty, cold, the water pressure is low or that the neighbours are noisy. You have to find out these things for yourself.

For longer tenancy agreements, particularly of older houses, a survey may be a worthwhile investment so that any problems can be written into the contract or repair or replacement arranged before the tenancy begins. This is particularly important if you are taking on a 'self-repairing' lease, which puts the responsibility for maintenance and repairs on to the tenant.

Before viewing a property for rent you will probably have already ascertained that the flat/house meets your requirements including:

■ rent – is it affordable/within your budget?

■ size – either the whole property or your room and the total size of the property if you are sharing;

■ location – near to or within easy travelling distance from work.

The initial inspection/viewing should tell you instantly if the property is suitable. Check:

■ the quality of decor;

■ the quality of furniture, fixtures and fittings;

■ what items are included/what items will be removed before you start to rent – such as the washing machine, dishwasher, kettle, TV, pictures, rugs, garden furniture. You don't want to move in and find that much of the furniture or fittings have been taken away by the previous tenant or by the landlord.

It is often at this stage that tenants agree to rent a property. But you do need to make additional investigations. Before agreeing to rent a property check the following by inspecting the flat or by asking the landlord or letting agent:

- Security: adequate locks, outside lighting, solid front door, etc.

- Safety: smoke alarms, fire exits, whether gas appliances have been maintained correctly and that furniture meets safety standards.

- Ventilation: will the bathroom or kitchen steam up because there are no windows?

- Extra costs: council tax can be expensive in some areas. Check the usual costs of heating and electricity – inefficient systems cost more.

- Insurance: the landlord usually arranges insurance for fixtures and furnishings that are provided with the flat, but what about your own belongings? Insurance can be expensive in some areas. Check the landlord's policy to find out what is covered and what you are liable for.

- Heating: how is the property heated, how does the system work and has it been serviced recently?

- Water: check the system by running taps, flushing the toilet and testing the shower for water pressure.

- Wiring: check that this is safe (it is not an obvious DIY job). Also check the number of electrical points.

- Test the furniture and fittings. You may find that the sofa has loose springs, the bed is about to collapse or there is a wobbly chair. All these should be noted on the inventory or you may be liable to replace or repair them when you leave the property.

- Rules: are there rules about pets, parties and noise levels after a certain hour?

▌ Your own possessions: are you allowed to put up your own pictures, bring in your own furniture?

▌ Decor: are you allowed to redecorate (this will apply particularly to those renting cheaper properties with poor decor or those planning to rent a property for a considerable amount of time)?

▌ Does the landlord have permission to sublet? You may be renting from someone who does not have the right to rent out the property.

Then make the following additional checks by viewing the property at different times and finding out as much as possible about the area:

▌ Noise – if you are viewing at a weekend you may be unaware that during the week the area is very noisy or you may find that you have noisy or undesirable neighbours.

▌ Transport – not only the distance to and from local transport facilities but the reliability and quality of service of buses, trains or tubes.

▌ Local facilities – if you work long hours you don't want to return to your new home only to find that there are no shops open.

▌ Parking – if you have a car, make sure that you will be able to park it, that you will qualify for a resident's parking permit or that it is safe to leave your car parked on the street.

Remember, it is your responsibility to check and double check. For instance, the advertisement may say parking is available. If you don't view the parking space you may not realize that it is too small to park your car in or that the car park is several hundred yards away.

2 Rental agreements and deposits

Rental agreements

Once you have found a property that suits your needs and meets your requirements you should then examine the rental agreement to make sure you are happy with the terms and conditions it imposes.

If you are planning to rent a flat or house in most cases you will usually have to take out a 'shorthold tenancy' and sign a tenancy agreement. This protects the landlord from sitting tenants.

Tenancies usually run for an initial period of six months, after which they may be renewable. The amended Housing Act introduced in the spring of 1997 means that assured shorthold tenancies no longer need to last for a minimum period of six months or be for a specified period of time. However, you can still agree on a six-month or one-year tenancy

For those wanting to rent for longer periods there is an 'assured longhold tenancy' agreement.

Most tenancy agreements comply with the Housing Act, although the exact wording can vary from agent to agent, with some letting agents inserting extra clauses to cover specific aspects of the property or area. If you are renting directly from a landlord, he or she will usually use a standard printed agreement bought from a legal stationers.

Remember, the tenancy agreement is a legally binding document between you and the landlord and as such you should read it carefully before signing. It should state:

- the address of the property;

- the amount of rent and to whom it is payable;

- length/term of tenancy;

- when rent is payable and what it includes/excludes;

- your rights and responsibilities (from a ban on pets to a requirement to leave the property clean at the end of the tenancy);

- the amount of the deposit and to whom it is payable;

- notice periods that both you and the landlord must give to terminate the agreement;

- bills that you are responsible for (for instance council tax/ gas/electricity/telephone/TV licence);

- there may also be security requirements. For instance you may be required to ensure that the property is left secure at all times. You may also be required to give the person managing the property written notice if you plan to be away from the property for more than 7, 14 or 30 days;

- you may also be told that you cannot change the locks or install any additional ones without the written consent of the landlord;

- there will usually be numerous other conditions which you should read carefully.

Rental agreements often stipulate that the landlord can enter and take possession of the property if you breach your tenancy agreement. However, landlords must usually apply to the courts before doing so.

Some agreements also state that the landlord is not liable for any injury suffered by tenants, even if this is caused by a defect on the premises or by neglect. However, tenants can normally make a civil claim against the landlord if, for instance, they are injured as a result of faulty wiring or a dangerous gas boiler.

When you sign your tenancy agreement you may also have to sign a 'Notice Requiring Possession (Assured Shorthold Tenancy)' or a 'Recovery of Possession of Dwelling' form which gives advance notice that you will vacate the property on a set date when the tenancy ends. Under the Housing Act this form protects the landlord and means that should the tenant fail to leave on the stated date or fail to pay the rent a court order for possession can be obtained more quickly.

When you sign the agreement you will usually be required to have your signature witnessed before an independent witness who should sign giving his or her name, address and occupation.

References

Landlords usually require references to ensure that you are who you say you are and can afford to pay the rent. As a result the landlord or letting agent may ask your permission to contact your bank or employer. You may also be asked to provide references from current and previous landlords. Not all landlords check references, but you should be prepared for them to do so and as such should make sure you alert all referees.

If you are using a professional letting agent you should expect them to conduct more thorough checks on prospective tenants.

If you are using a letting agent then that agent will usually write to your bank or building society to confirm your ability to meet the rental commitment. They may also ask if they can contact your employer. Agents may also check your credit rating with a credit reference agency to find out if you have any county court judgements against you for non-payment of debts.

It is essential that you are honest as the new Housing Act introduced in early 1997 allows landlords to evict tenants who gain a tenancy by knowingly providing false information.

Making your own checks

You may not want to go as far as asking your landlord for references, but you should still undertake your own checks. It has been known for landlords to rent out property when they are not entitled to do so. For instance, they may be in default on their rent/mortgage, may not be the legal tenant of the property or may not have permission to sublet. You could hand over the deposit and first month's rent only to find that the property is about to be repossessed.

Deposits

In most cases you will be required to pay between a month and six weeks' rent as a deposit to cover any damage to the property or the furniture, fixtures and fittings. The deposit also covers any costs incurred by the landlord to clean or make good the property after the tenancy ends. The deposit is not refundable until you vacate – or for two to three weeks after you leave – the property. The delay may be while the landlord gets estimates for or pays for repairs, replacement of items or for cleaning.

If you are renting through a reputable letting agent, the deposit will normally be held in an account run by the agent. You will need to make sure that the money is protected in case the agent goes bust or absconds with your money. If you are giving the deposit directly to the landlord there may be even less protection. To avoid losing your deposit ask the following questions:

If using a letting agent or estate agent:

▌ Will the deposit be held in a separate account?

▌ Can the agent get access to funds held in that account or is the money protected in any way?

▌ Does the agent require the signature of both the tenant and the landlord to release the deposit? This will prevent the landlord from keeping your deposit at the end of the tenancy.

Letting agents do not have to hold deposits in a separate account unless they are members of a trade body (such as the Association of Residential Letting Agents). Check first – not all letting agents are professional.

If paying a deposit to a landlord:

■ Where will the deposit be held? If it is in the landlord's bank account you may have difficulty in getting it returned and certainly won't earn interest. Occasionally landlords open a separate account and give the tenant the interest at the end of the tenancy. But this is very rare.

■ Will the landlord allow you to open a joint account that requires both the landlord's and the tenant's signature before the money can be withdrawn? This way neither you nor the landlord can get access to the deposit without mutual agreement. And if you open an interest-bearing account you can split the interest.

Always make sure you are given a receipt for your deposit to prove you have made the payment. Keep a note of who you paid the deposit to and when.

If you are renting through a reputable agent, your deposit may be protected. For example, the Association of Residential Letting Agents (ARLA) offers a Fidelity Bond. This is designed as a protection of first resort for monies entrusted to ARLA members by landlords and tenants during the ordinary course of their business as letting agents.

In the event of proven theft or fraud of client monies by a member agent or its staff and if the agent's own insurance does not cover the loss, you may make a claim to ARLA for reimbursement of the money you have lost.

This will not cover every situation. Often landlords simply keep the deposits and see it as a way of making extra money. According to research from The National Association of Citizens Advice Bureaux, half of private tenants believe they have had a deposit unreasonably withheld. Of those, around two-thirds lose either all or part of the deposit.

Of course, it is possible to take a landlord to the small claims court to retrieve the deposit. However, work by Shelter suggests that this can be expensive and time-consuming. As a result there has been pressure for a change in the law.

Warning: One of the most common problems faced by renters – affecting one in five – is getting their deposit returned at the end of the tenancy. Half are never told why their deposit – usually one month's rent – is not returned.

For the others, the landlord often claims to have a good reason to withhold the money often saying that the money was used to pay for cleaning of the property or damage to furniture and carpets. To avoid this being a problem, when vacating a property check through the inventory very carefully with either the landlord or the specialist agency employed by the landlord and agree what level of repairs/cleaning needs to be done. Then, if there is a dispute, you have written proof of what was agreed.

Legal changes to the way deposits are held

A national tenancy deposit scheme to protect the £800 million of tenants' money held by landlords has been proposed by the charity Shelter and the Citizens Advice Bureaux.

They want the scheme to be included in the forthcoming Housing Bill and, although at the time of writing it was not yet included, a select committee report has also recommended that the scheme be included in the Bill.

Legislation seems a possibility, as a pilot voluntary deposit scheme launched by the government in March 2000 and managed by the independent housing ombudsman failed to take off and attracted only minimal participation by landlords.

Making the payments

In cases where payment of the first month's rent and the deposit are required quickly you will have to pay either by cash or by banker's draft. Always make sure you receive a receipt as proof of payment.

3 Moving in

You can usually move in at 12 noon: the same time applies to vacating the property. Prior to moving into a property you should notify the following:

- The relevant utility services – they should be told of a change of occupier and you should ask for the meters to be read. This is so that you are not charged for outstanding bills or for any electricity or gas used prior to the date that you move in.

- Your bank, building society, tax office and any other savings and investment companies.

- Your employer.

- The Post Office – if you want mail forwarded from a previous address.

- The council, so that you can start paying council tax.

- The TV licensing authority.

- British Telecom – or other telephone service provider.

- A local doctor/dentist – so you can register as a patient.

- The local council, if you want to apply for a parking permit.

The inventory

If you are renting through a professional letting agent, the agent will normally employ a firm to take an inventory at the start of the tenancy and at the end. If this is not done, you should make your own list and get the landlord to sign this.

The inventory should not only include all furniture, fittings, linen, crockery and other items but should also state their condition. For instance if the carpet has stains on it, a wooden table is scratched or the curtains have not been dry cleaned, make sure a note is made of this. If you don't, when you vacate the property you may find that you are charged for cleaning the carpets and curtains or for repairing damaged furniture even though it was in this condition when you first started to rent the property.

Warning: When you leave the property there will usually be a requirement that the property is thoroughly cleaned and that all items of furniture are in the same condition as at the start of the tenancy and are returned to their original location in the property. If you fail to meet these requirements you will probably be charged for cleaning or repairs and as a result the landlord may not return your deposit. If you do not have a detailed inventory you may find it hard to prove that you left the property in the same condition that you found it.

The check-in

Make sure the inventory is checked at the time you actually move in and that both you and the landlord/landlord's agent sign the check-in report. This should include checking the inventory to ensure the contents, furniture and fixtures are as described in the inventory.

Either make sure the inventory covers the condition of the property and its contents or make out your own list and ask that the landlord/landlord's agent signs this. It should include:

■ General condition: is it clean?

■ Decorative order: if there are any defects, damp stains, peeling wallpaper, etc, make sure this is noted or the landlord may claim that you are liable.

■ Carpets/flooring: note if they have been cleaned or not and make a list of any marks.

■ Curtains/upholstery: again make a note of any marks/defects and also find out if they have been cleaned before the start of the tenancy as you may be required to pay for professional cleaning before vacating the property.

■ Furniture: note any marks, stains or scratches.

■ Kitchen equipment: check if any items are chipped or cracked. Again, if you don't make a note of this at the start of the tenancy you may find that you are liable to replace these items when your tenancy ends. If they are part of a set you may find individual items hard to replace and may have to buy a whole new set.

■ Lighting: check which lights are working and which are not.

■ Glazing: make sure that there are no defects.

Meter readings: Although you will have to ask the utility companies to check meter readings when you move in, you should also get the landlord/landlord's agent to agree the meter reading at the start of the tenancy to ensure you are not charged for usage prior to the date you move in.

Keys: You should also have in writing the number of keys that you are supplied with.

Keep a copy of your check-in report along with your inventory.

Moving out

As most private renters now have assured shorthold tenancy agreements, they often know when their tenancy will end – or can be renewed. This is usually six months or one year.

A landlord may seek automatic possession of a property let on an assured shorthold tenancy after six months has elapsed or, where a longer fixed term was agreed, at the end of that fixed term. At least two months' notice of his or her intention to seek possession is required to be served on the tenant.

If a tenant does not leave at the end of the notice period, a landlord must apply to a county court for a possession order. Normally, there are no grounds for a tenant to contest a possession application under an assured shorthold tenancy and the court may grant an order without arranging a formal hearing. Once a possession order has been granted, a tenant must leave and can be evicted by bailiffs if they do not.

If you wish to leave, you must give the required amount of notice. However, bear in mind that you may be required to rent the property for a minimum of six months.

In addition, the landlord can seek possession of the property earlier by starting legal proceedings if you breach the agreement – for example, you are in arrears on your rent.

Before leaving make sure you comply with the agreement. You will need to clean the property including getting all linen, used or not, freshly laundered. If you have moved furniture, return it to where you found it at the time of the inventory. You may even need to replace light bulbs and have the windows cleaned. After an inventory check and condition inspection, provided there are no missing items or damage, your deposit should be returned shortly after you leave the property. You cannot usually set your deposit against the last rent payment due.

4 Legal aspects, maintenance and problems

Renting and the law

Recent legislation has given more protection to landlords against sitting tenants, but has also increased the protection of tenants against unscrupulous landlords.

What your landlord can and cannot do

Landlords cannot:

■ enter a tenant's property without permission unless it is an absolute emergency;

■ change the locks without the tenant's permission.

Landlords can:

■ enter the property to inspect it or for maintenance and repairs, but only if they give reasonable notice;

■ require that you undertake repairs you are responsible for, and if you do not do so within the specified time period the landlord can enter the premises to make the repairs and then charge you for them;

■ enter the property in the last few weeks of the tenancy to show other prospective tenants round the property;

▌ charge you if you fail to keep an appointment to check the inventory at the end of the tenancy;

▌ charge interest if you are late in paying the rent.

Fire and safety regulations

Fire

When renting a property it is essential to check that the landlord meets all requirements for health and safety. Although there are laws in place, some unscrupulous landlords have rented out death traps in the past where faulty wiring has caused fires, a lack of fire escapes has led to the death of tenants, or faulty gas boilers have exploded.

Under the legislation, which came into force on 1 January 1997, landlords letting furnished property have to ensure that furniture has fire retardant fillings. All upholstery, fillings and covers must have passed flammability tests and be labelled accordingly. Landlords must remove 'non-compliant' furniture prior to letting or face a fine of up to £5,000 or up to six months in prison. Most furniture sold since 1990 should comply, but you should ask to see fire retardant information and check the landlord has safety certificates. If the landlord is renting out his or her own home for a temporary period and not in the course of his or her business, then there is a moral rather than a legal responsibility to comply.

If the landlord fails to meet these requirements and there is a fire you may be able to make a claim for civil damages against the landlord.

New homes built after June 1992 must have smoke detectors installed on every floor.

Gas

The landlord must also ensure that a safety check of any gas appliance is carried out every 12 months by an approved person who must be CORGI registered. A record must be kept of all safety inspections and their results and this must be given to the tenant. Even if the landlord has asked for gas appliances – for instance the boiler – to be serviced this may not be sufficient as the safety check must include set information.

The regulations cover all gas appliances including mains gas, propane gas and calor gas.

Electricity

Again, the landlord must ensure that all electrical appliances and the electrical supply are safe and will not cause any danger. All new electrical appliances must carry a 'CE' mark and instruction booklets or clear working instructions must be given to tenants.

Health and safety

In order for a property to be considered a fit place to live it has to meet a fitness standard. However, there has been a consensus that this standard fails to meet modern health and safety hazards and risks and focuses too much on housing conditions.

The government has proposed a new system, the Housing Health and Safety Rating System (HHSRS), which is now being adopted by local authorities and will be enforced by Environmental Health Officers who can take action, for example by issuing an improvement notice. The HHSRS is expected to form part of the new Housing Act.

Licensing of landlords

Many local authorities run voluntary registration schemes for landlords in their areas and these will be extended if the new legislation is introduced. It will also stop landlords holding deposits – something that causes many tenants problems as they find it hard to get them returned when they leave the property. In future – as in many cases already – the deposit will either be held in a secure account by the letting agent or in a joint account requiring the signature of both the tenant and landlord.

If you are thinking of renting find out if your local council runs one of these schemes. The new rules will require landlords to meet basic health and safety standards.

The new Housing Act

The rights of tenants should be further strengthened when a new Housing Act is introduced in the next few years.

In 2001 the Law Commission was asked to review the law regulating landlords and occupiers, which over the last 100 years has become exceedingly complex. This report should form the basis of the new legislation.

The Act will improve controls on Houses in Multiple Occupation (HMOs). This will include a mandatory national licensing scheme, to tackle poor physical and management standards and to give local authorities powers to license all landlords in areas of low housing demand where the growth and poor management of the private rented sector frustrates efforts to create sustainable communities.

The Act is also likely to include model agreements for use by landlords that are fair, easy to read and understand and set out clearly the rights and obligations of both landlords and tenants.

Type I agreements for use by social landlords will offer a high degree of security of tenure. Type II agreements will be for private landlords with the security of tenure determined largely by the agreement.

All occupation agreements should come under the scope of the scheme – including existing agreements.

Landlords who fail to provide written agreements will face fines.

Agreements will have four types of term:

Key terms – providing information about the property, the landlord, the tenant and the rent.

Compulsory-minimum terms – which will:
1. prescribe the circumstances in which the landlord can seek possession against the occupier;
2. set down the duties imposed by law on landlords (such as statutory repairing obligations). These can be changed – by mutual agreement – but only in favour of the occupier.

Special terms – which impose obligations on occupiers for social policy reasons (particularly regarding antisocial behaviour).

Other terms – These will deal with other issues needed to make the contract work and set out in the model agreements and any substitute terms agreed to by both the landlord and tenant.

Due process: The principle of due process where a landlord can only get lawful possession of a property with a court order will be retained. In addition, landlords will have to first give notice of the intention to take proceedings. However, in the case of antisocial behaviour this notice can be issued at the same time as court proceedings begin.

Sharing a rented property: The new agreements will make it easier for you to know where you stand legally.

For example:

■ You rent a property on your own but then want to move your partner into the property.

■ A group of friends rent the property together but then fall out and one wants to leave and another person wants to move in.

The new law is likely to require the consent of the landlord for any change but set out the requirements more clearly.

Joint occupation: You are jointly liable for any rent or rent arrears – which means that even if you have paid your half of the rent you are also liable for the other half.

This will remain the situation even when the law changes.

A joint occupier will, however, be able to leave the property (after giving the required notice) without the entire agreement coming to an end. So the other occupier should be able to continue living in the property under the same agreement and terms.

Taking in a lodger: If you need help to pay the rent you will be able, as a Type I occupier, to take in a lodger without having to get the consent of the landlord (unless your agreement specifically excludes this). Type II occupiers will have to get the consent of the landlord.

Once you have moved in

What you must do

Abide by the tenancy agreement or else you could face eviction. Your agreement may include dozens of small clauses, but you should be aware of all of them even if they only stipulate that you must weed the garden.

Some tenancy agreements go into great detail including, for example, requirements that:

■ you do not alter the layout of the garden without the previous consent in writing of the landlord;

■ you wash all net curtains at least every six weeks;

■ you do not play any musical instruments or use any sound equipment that causes an annoyance or disturbance to adjoining residents;

■ you do not take in lodgers (so if your boyfriend/girlfriend moves in tell the landlord first);

■ you report any faults or damage to the landlord before repairs or replacement so that the landlord can authorize the repairs or claim on his or her insurance policy.

Also note that many tenancy agreements require you to inform the person managing the property should you be away from the property for more than seven consecutive days. This is not only to ensure security, but also so that the agent can check that there are no frozen pipes or other problems during your absence.

Repairs and maintenance

If the property is managed – either by the landlord or an agent – it should mean that you do not have to worry about maintenance or ongoing repairs. However, in some cases there are a few repairs that the tenant must do.

In a legal ruling, Lord Denning put it like this:

'The tenant must take proper care of the premises ... he must do the little jobs around the house which a reasonable tenant will do.'

So things like changing lightbulbs, replacing fuses, day-to-day maintenance of electrical items (defrosting the fridge, keeping the washing machine clear of blockages) and keeping the sink clear of blockages will probably be the tenant's – not the landlord's – responsibility. If you are unsure you should make sure both you and your landlord agree in advance what management services will be provided. If you read your tenancy agreement carefully you should find that your responsibilities are explained – although this may be in 'legalese' rather than plain English.

Wear and tear clauses in most tenancy agreements require that all electrical appliances are kept in good repair by the landlord. So if the fridge or washing machine breaks down a replacement does not have to be found immediately. The landlord has 'a reasonable time' in which to arrange for repairs and no compensation for the loss of this appliance needs to be paid to the tenant.

What landlords are responsible for

They are responsible for most repairs including repairs to the structure of the property and sanitary, heating and hot water installations. However, landlords are not normally responsible for repairs resulting from wilful damage by tenants.

It is very important that the landlord has used a CORGI-registered gas installer to inspect all gas appliances annually. It is a criminal offence not to have a valid gas safety certificate for any gas appliance in a rented property.

Renting and insurance

If you rent a furnished property you are advised to insure anything which belongs to you. If you are burgled and all that is stolen is your television, video and some cash, the insurance provided by your landlord will not cover your loss. Most tenancy agreements state that you must insure your own personal effects.

Most leases specify that the landlord's responsibility only covers the furniture and fittings. Check that it does or else you may be liable for loss of your landlord's possessions as well.

If you are renting a property, you may find that insurance is expensive or difficult to obtain. If you have difficulties, contact an insurance broker, who can shop around for a suitable policy on your behalf.

Dealing with problems

Buying a property is supposed to be one of the most stressful things in your life, along with death, divorce and redundancy.

Renting does not even make it to the top 10 in the stress list. However, for some it can be a fraught process. Even if you are in the right, getting redress or compensation can be difficult. Here are the most common types of dispute and how to deal with them:

■ The landlord refuses to sort out a problem/repair or asks you to sort it out, even though it is not your responsibility:

Read your tenancy agreement carefully. It will normally state that you must inform your landlord immediately and in writing if there is 'any damage, disrepair, defect or deficiency'. So make sure all correspondence is in writing and you keep copies of it. Also make sure you report problems – for instance, a leaking pipe – as soon as possible or you may be liable for any further damage. Find out if the problem/repair is covered by the landlord's insurance – if you can prove it will not cost anything, the landlord is more likely to agree to repairs.

Don't undertake any repairs yourself or pay a workman to do them for you unless you get written permission to do so from your landlord and an agreement that the landlord will pay the bill. It is not unknown for landlords to not only refuse to pay for the repairs but also to charge for leaving the premises in a poorer condition than before because – or so they claim – the repairs were not of sufficient quality.

■ The landlord continually pops in to check the flat/enters the flat when you are not there:

Most tenancy agreements stipulate that the landlord must give you written notice before entering the property. You should point this out without trying to antagonize the landlord. Do not change the locks to prevent the landlord entering the flat as you will probably be in breach of your tenancy agreement.

■ You lose your job and can no longer pay the rent:

The new Housing Act introduced in the spring of 1997 makes it easier for landlords to regain possession if you fail to pay the rent. They can apply to the courts after only two months and claim unpaid rent. If you get into difficulties it is essential that you claim benefits as soon as possible. But be warned, social security will not cover rent on a luxury apartment.

■ The landlord refuses to return your deposit:

Either complain to the letting agent (if you used one) or threaten to take your landlord to court. Often landlords believe that they are allowed to charge you for repairs/cleaning, even though you believe you have left the property in good order and as clean as you found it.

Often the dispute is over what is 'wear and tear' and what is 'damage'. You will normally have to pay for repair or replacement of any items which have been damaged during the tenancy, but not for 'fair wear and tear'. Your landlord can tax deduct around 10 per cent of the rent to cover 'wear and tear', which covers deterioration due to normal usage. The landlord may refuse to return the deposit, claiming damage to furniture or that the property was not left in the same condition as at the start of the tenancy. If you take your case to the small claims court it is vital that you have evidence – the inventory and any relevant photographs.

Some landlords keep the deposit to pay for redecoration so that they can spruce up the flat/house before new tenants move in. But if you left the flat in good decorative order and did not leave any marks on the walls or tear any wallpaper you should not have to pay for this.

If the landlord refuses to pay back the deposit, and you do not agree with his or her reasons, you may have to take out a summons in the small claims court. This is the cheapest form of legal redress. It can deal with claims for up to £5,000 (in England and Wales), although the maximum claim in housing disrepair cases is only £1,000. Ask at your local county court (or sheriff's court in Scotland) for details. You do not need a lawyer and the hearings are relatively informal. The court fees range from £20 to £100, depending on the amount of money you are claiming. If you lose your case the most you have to pay is the other side's expenses for attending the hearing. Information is available from Citizens Advice Bureaux and county or sheriff's courts.

Complaining

If you have a complaint about your landlord or the property the first step is to write to your landlord. Keep the tone of the letter pleasant but firm. Clearly state what the problem is and refer to your tenancy agreement to show your landlord that you know your rights. Keep copies of all correspondence. Avoid losing your temper as this will only antagonize the landlord.

If you still have no joy you can pursue your complaint in the following ways:

■ If you have rented through an Association of Residential Letting Agents (ARLA) member you may be able to take your case to the association's arbitration service.

■ Contact your local Citizens Advice Bureau for advice. They will help you write letters and will usually negotiate on your behalf.

■ If you are seeking compensation – for instance the return of your deposit – you can, as a last resort, take your landlord to court.

£ CASH TIP £

Consider taking out legal expenses insurance. Stand-alone policies can be expensive but you may find that for just £1 a month you can buy this cover as part of your home contents or motor insurance policy or that you get it free as part of your membership of a trade union or professional body. This insurance will usually provide you with a legal helpline which will give you advice and help you write legal letters.

For further information:

The Office of the Deputy Prime Minister produces several free guides on tenancy issues for landlords and tenants, all of which can be downloaded from the Web site www.odpm.gov.uk – see 'Booklets for Landlords and Tenants Renting Privately' for the full range.

Alternatively, all of the booklets can be ordered, free of charge, from:

ODPM Free Literature
PO Box 236
Wetherby
West Yorkshire, LS23 7NB

Tel: 0870 1226 236

5 From renter to buyer

Making the move from being a renter to being a buyer is getting harder. The average first-time buyer, now aged 33, has to save almost £20,000 as a deposit while paying for day-to-day living costs, rent (which is often equivalent to a mortgage) and often having to repay student loans.

So how can a renter make the move to being a buyer, when already suffering the expense of paying rent?

Help from family and friends

The obvious option is to move back home or move in with friends to reduce the rent you pay and enable you to save up a deposit more quickly.

Other alternatives are:

■ asking your parents to act as a guarantor to help you take out a larger mortgage;

■ asking your parents to buy the property jointly – they then have an investment in a second property and you can afford a home;

■ buying with a friend/family member so that you can pool resources.

Help from housing associations

Those who cannot afford to buy can consider shared ownership schemes. These enable you to part-rent and part-buy a home. Offered by Housing Associations these are usually only offered to those who:

- cannot afford to buy a home without assistance;
- can demonstrate they will be able to sustain homeownership;
- are first-time buyers.

Some schemes are restricted to key workers.

You will have to register with a Housing Association and wait on a list, if your application is approved.

Through shared ownership you buy a share of the property and pay a rent on the remaining share you do not own. Gradually you may buy further shares and eventually own your home outright.

Remember that house prices tend to rise. This means that you might pay far more for buying additional shares.

Priority will normally be given to existing public sector tenants or those on local authority or social landlords' waiting lists.

Although you have not bought the property outright, you will have the normal rights and responsibilities of a full owner-occupier.

Shared ownership homes may be new or renovated flats or houses that are sold by social landlords. Prices vary according to location but are expected to be within the means of those people who cannot afford the prices of properties available for sale in the open market.

How does shared ownership work?

The scheme allows you to purchase a share of a property from a social landlord, usually a housing association. The share you purchase is funded by a mortgage that you will need to arrange with a bank or building society. The remaining share you do not own is rented from the social landlord.

The size of the share to be purchased will depend on your income and savings. Normally applicants buy a 50 per cent share but you may purchase a smaller or larger share (to start with, you can buy as little as 25 per cent or as much as 75 per cent). The higher the share you purchase the less rent you will have to pay.

You will also have to pay a service charge when you buy a flat. Later on, if you wish and can afford to do so, you can buy a further share.

When you purchase through shared ownership, the social landlord will grant you a lease that sets out your rights and responsibilities.

If your home is a house, you will be responsible for all repairs and redecoration both internally and externally. The social landlord will insure the structure of your home and you will have to pay a small management charge to cover this and to help meet the costs of rent collection. If your home is a flat, you will be responsible for all repairs and redecoration internally. The social landlord will undertake to keep the building in which your flat is situated in good structural repair, to keep the structure insured and to keep any common parts, such as the staircase and corridors, decorated, cleaned and lighted. You will have to pay a share of those costs. This is called a service charge. The social landlord must tell you how the service charge is spent and you will be consulted before any major repair or maintenance work is put in hand.

There are special mortgages for shared ownership purchasers available from major lenders. Some social landlords offer non-government-funded shared ownership schemes that work on the same principles but some details may vary. Also, a few private developers offer shared ownership schemes where a wide range of conditions apply.

Existing tenants of social landlords and those on housing waiting lists can also get help with purchasing their home through the Right to Acquire, HomeBuy and Right to Buy Schemes.

Help from the government

The government's intention to offer some form of help to first-time buyers is clear. Concerned that those on modest incomes will be unable to buy their own homes it launched a Task Force on Home Ownership to look into this problem. The task force came up with 45 proposals. See www.housingcorplibrary.org.uk for more information.

First-time buyers will have to wait for the new Housing Act to benefit from some of the proposals to improve affordability as these are yet to be finalized. In future developments – particularly in areas where homes are less affordable – will probably have to include a set percentage that are affordable.

The Sustainable Home Ownership Programme, championed by the Housing Corporation, will offer three opportunities: ownership discounts, equity loans and shared ownership.

The Starter Home Initiative, a government-funded scheme to help key workers, primarily teachers, health workers and the police, to buy a home in areas where high house prices are undermining recruitment and retention, ended in March 2004. The scheme was available in London, the South East and housing hot spots in Eastern and South Western England. It will be succeeded by a new key worker programme due to start on 1 April 2004 which will focus more on those delivering frontline public services, such as health workers and teachers, where there are significant recruitment and retention issues. It will extend housing assistance to key workers at different life-stages, not just first-time buyers.

Around 6,000 key workers are expected to be helped in each of its first two years – 2004/05 and 2005/06 in London, the South East and Eastern regions.

There will also be a small key worker scheme in the South West. Four products will be available:

■ Homebuy – which provides an equity loan of at least 25 per cent of the property value up to a limit of £50,000;

- London Challenge Key Teacher Homebuy – providing a higher loan value limit for which only a small, highly targeted group of teachers will be eligible;

- Intermediate renting – a rent between social and open market rates (basically subsidised rents);

- Shared ownership on new build schemes, where the purchaser buys a share of the equity from a minimum of 25 per cent and pays rent on the balance.

At the time of writing the full scheme details, including a list of eligible key worker groups, was yet to be announced. It is likely that all public sector workers in areas where house prices cause problems with recruitment or retention are likely to be eligible. Some £1 billion is likely to be available.

Some housing association schemes also help social workers, care workers, firefighters, transport workers, occupational therapists and a limited number of prison and probation staff.

Help includes equity loans and shared ownership and most schemes allow the buyer to purchase a property on the open market although some involve the buyer purchasing a new-built property being provided through the scheme (usually run by a housing association). First-time buyers should keep watch on these types of schemes as they could even affect career choices.

Visit www.odpm.gov.uk – the Office of the Deputy Prime Minister – for information on scheme providers and progress on the implementation of these new initiatives. The Housing Corporation at www.housingcorp.gov.uk also has useful information on Shared Ownership and other housing initiatives.

Help from a housebuilder

Housebuilders, keen to sell to first-time buyers, will often help with the deposit, give cash back to help fund the costs of purchase, throw in free curtains and carpets (and even furniture) and help with legal costs. However, remember that they are in business to make money. You will end up paying for this help in a higher property price.

In the past some builders offered part-ownership schemes where purchasers buy, for example, 75 per cent of the property, and agree to buy the remaining 25 per cent at a later date. These are not offered widely any longer. However, if the number of first-time buyers continues to dry up and affects the property market, these schemes could be reintroduced.

Part 2 Buying

The first few chapters of this section look at the things you need to do before you start house-hunting. You should talk to a mortgage lender about the size of home loan you can afford to borrow and how much deposit you will need, and then start to look for a solicitor who will handle the conveyancing.

This is essential in the current property market. Many estate agents will not treat you as a serious buyer unless you already have finance in place. In addition, properties often sell very quickly. If you cannot complete the sale within a few weeks you are at risk of being 'gazumped' – when another buyer offers a higher price and as a result you lose the property and all the fees you have spent on surveyors and conveyancing.

6 Mortgages

Choosing the right mortgage to meet your needs is just as important as picking the right property. But while it may take you months to find the home you want to buy, the chances are that you will put comparatively little thought into selecting a home loan.

It is only when you compare the different interest costs over the life-time of the mortgage that you realize just how much you can save by shopping around for the best mortgage deal.

But with more than 1,000 different mortgage products on offer at any one time, it can be very difficult to decide which will offer you the best value. The interest payable on a standard variable-rate mortgage can vary considerably from one mortgage lender to another. It is very much to your advantage, therefore, to spend time comparing what's on offer to ensure that you choose the best-value lender.

First-time buyers account for a sizeable chunk of mortgage lending and as such are in a powerful position to negotiate a good rate and shop around. Many lenders offer preferential rates or special offers to first-time buyers, so make the most of these.

When you should arrange a mortgage

In the current property market it is advisable to agree your mortgage in advance of looking for properties so that you know what you can afford. Often estate agents will want to know you have finance arranged before showing you properties. And if you have a mortgage prearranged you will reduce the risk of being gazumped.

Although you do not need to agree to a particular size of mortgage (this may be difficult as you will not yet know how much you want to borrow), you should arrange the maximum loan that you qualify for 'in principle'. This means that you have applied for the mortgage and the lender has agreed to advance the home loan on certain conditions:

■ your circumstances do not change;

■ the property is suitable security for the mortgage;

■ you have a sufficient deposit;

■ you meet all the other terms and conditions.

Who to approach for a mortgage

The days when you had to queue for a mortgage from your local building society are long over. You no longer have the choice of just a bank or building society. Insurance companies, centralized lenders, telephone-based or direct mortgage companies, mortgage advice centres, mortgage brokers and even super-markets all offer home loans. Surveys have shown that the smaller, local building societies tend to offer cheaper mortgages over the longer term, but they do restrict who they will lend to. Whoever you decide to take a mortgage with, look at that lender's long-term mortgage record to:

■ ensure that its rates are consistently competitive;

■ check that the lender passes on rate reductions quickly;

■ ensure that the lender is not one of the first to up its mortgage rates when interest rates rise.

Your bank and/or building society

You could approach these first. As you are already a customer and may have saved up a deposit in one of their accounts, they are more likely to consider you for a mortgage.

Another bank or building society

You do not have to have a bank or savings account with a lender to take out a mortgage – although if you don't have one, you will usually be asked to open one if you take out a loan.

A telephone/direct lender

More lenders are offering loans by phone or Internet. This means you can get an agreement on a loan very quickly. However, you will not be able to sit down and work through all the figures with the adviser.

A mortgage broker/financial adviser/estate agent

Approaching these first has the advantage of saving you time. If you went to a building society, bank or direct lender you would receive advice only on the mortgage loans offered by that society, bank or direct lender. Mortgage brokers have access to a wide variety of mortgage lenders although you may have to pay for this service. Mortgage brokers can also help those who may otherwise find it hard to get a mortgage. In some cases you may have to pay an arrangement fee – check if you will still have to pay this fee even if you do not go ahead or if the sale falls through.

The Internet

The Internet is fast becoming a major source of not only mortgage information but also mortgage lending, with online mortgage brokers and lenders often offering the best rates to those prepared to apply on the Internet. Half of all intermediary lending is now conducted online and this online lending accounts for a fifth of total UK gross mortgage lending.

Use the Internet to compare the best buys (try sites like www.moneysupermarket.com, www.charcolonline.co.uk and the government's comparative site at www.fsa.gov.uk).

Mortgage regulation

Despite the fact that taking out a mortgage is probably the biggest financial commitment any of us will make, mortgages – or rather the sale of mortgages – has not, until now, been regulated by the city watchdogs.

Only from 31 October 2004 will the Financial Services Authority (FSA) start to regulate the mortgage business.

Those selling mortgages have two choices:

1. to be directly authorized by the FSA;
2. to become an appointed representative of an authorized firm.

Designed to give better protection for consumers over the entire life of their mortgage, the new regulatory regime will require firms to:

■ provide consumers with clear, comparable information about the service they are receiving and the mortgage itself. This will make it easier to shop around and to make an informed decision;

■ identify the mortgage which best meets the customers' needs (when advice is given);

■ consider the homebuyer's ability to repay the loan;

■ meet new standards for dealing with borrowers who are in arrears or facing repossession. This includes sending out a new FSA information sheet explaining what the borrower's options are if they cannot meet their mortgage payment.

Until now, the sale of mortgages has been governed by a voluntary Mortgage Code.

Under the existing Mortgage Code lenders must recommend the most suitable product from their range and explain the reasons for recommending a particular mortgage in writing.

This should mean that if an endowment mortgage is not the best type of home loan for you, you should not be pushed into buying one.

However, you should be aware that lenders can opt out of the advice requirement by giving information only.

The code requires that:

▮ you are given full details of mortgage costs, including early redemption penalties;

▮ any requirement to buy insurance as part of the mortgage package must be explained;

▮ if you are taking out a fixed-rate or discounted mortgage, you will be shown how your repayments are likely to increase at the end of that period (based on the lender's current variable rate);

▮ if the lender is giving you advice it must recommend the most suitable mortgage from its range and state the reasons in writing;

▮ lenders must be members of an ombudsman or arbitration scheme to cover complaints.

However, if a lender only gives *information* not *advice*, the 'most suitable' rules do not apply. And even if the lender is giving advice, it does not have to ensure that the mortgage is completely suitable, only that it is the most suitable product that is offered by that lender. So if you need a mortgage that is more flexible and the lender does not offer this product, there is no requirement for the lender to tell you so.

How much can I borrow?

This is the first thing you need to know so that you can start looking for properties in your price bracket. Generally you will be required to put down a deposit of at least 5 per cent of the purchase price, although it is possible to take out a 100 per cent home loan which requires no deposit at all.

To get the best deals, you will generally need a much larger deposit of up to 25 per cent of the purchase price. So if you are buying a £50,000 property, you will need a deposit of £12,500.

Generally you can borrow three times your annual salary if you are buying alone. If you are buying with a partner you can borrow up to 2.5 times your joint salary or three times the main salary plus the additional salary.

How much a couple with a joint income of £40,000 can borrow varies from £90,000 to £106,000:

1   Mr A earns £25,000 and Ms B earns £15,000
They can either borrow:

£75,000 (3 × £25,000) + £15,000	=	£90,000
or: 2.5 × £40,000 (£25,000 + £15,000)	=	£100,000

2   Mr A earns £33,000 and Ms B earns £7,000
They can either borrow:

£99,000 (3 × £33,000) + £7,000	=	£106,000
or: 2.5 × £40,000 (£33,000 + £7,000)	=	£100,000

Generally, if there is not a great difference between each buyer's salary the 2.5 × joint salary option is better. If one buyer earns significantly more, then the 3 × main income + the second salary calculation will qualify the homebuyers for a larger mortgage.

Boosting what you can borrow

Enhanced income multiples

More than 40 lenders offer what are known as enhanced income multiple mortgages – lending up to four times salary or three-and-a-half times joint income. These are often restricted to professionals.

In some cases borrowers are taking out loans of as much as six or even seven times their earnings – and even taking out extra loans to pay for their deposits. However borrowers often falsify their earnings taking out 'self-certification' mortgages which require no proof of income. In other cases lenders are prepared to extend borrowing limits to graduates and those in good jobs such as trainee solicitors where their salaries are expected to rise quickly.

Stepladder lending

This is a new type of loan that enables buyers to pay interest on only 70 per cent of the purchase price with the lender allowing the remaining 30 per cent to be interest-free. In return the lender takes a share of the increased property value.

What earnings can be taken into account?

The income you can take into account when working out how much you can borrow is your basic salary before tax and other deductions.

In addition, if part of your earnings are made up of commission or bonuses you may be able to add these to your salary to boost the amount you can borrow. However, your lender will want to see proof that these payments are consistent (if not guaranteed) and will probably require your employer to put this in writing.

If you are self-employed you will generally have to supply three years of audited accounts. The amount you can borrow will usually be based on your average earnings over that three-year period and you will have to supply accounts, tax assessments and sometimes a business plan showing that your future earnings are likely to be the same or greater than in the past. Those who have been self-employed for less than three years should opt for a 'self-certification' mortgage, which requires that you supply details of your income without having to provide proof.

What if you are new to your job?

Most lenders will want to know that your job is secure before advancing a mortgage. If you have been in your job for only a few months you may not yet have security of employment. As a result you represent a higher lending risk. Your lender may therefore require that you take out mortgage protection insurance to cover your mortgage repayments should you lose your job. However, read the small print as this may not cover you unless you have been employed for a minimum period.

What if you don't have a permanent employment contract?

Changing employment patterns mean that an increasing number of workers are no longer given full-time permanent employment. If you work on a contract basis you will probably find it difficult to get a home loan unless you have been consistently employed for the last three years, in which case you may be treated in a similar way to a self-employed borrower.

One option is to opt for a *self-certification mortgage*. These are designed for those who are self-employed and contract workers, and borrowers do not require proof of income. Generally the loan must not be more than 75 to 90 per cent of the property's value. However, these loans can come at a price, with interest rates often 0.5 or 1 per cent above the standard variable rate. You will often have to go to a mortgage broker – who may charge a fee of 1 per cent of the loan – to arrange this type of mortgage.

Using a guarantor to increase the amount you can borrow

If you have a temporary contract, are not in secure employment or do not have enough earnings to borrow the amount you need you can ask a friend or relative (usually your parents) to act as a guarantor.

If you cannot meet the payments they will then become liable. The lender will want to know that the guarantor has sufficient income or equity in their own property to meet your repayments or repay the outstanding loan.

Getting your parents to help

Increasingly parents are helping their children onto the property ladder.

The traditional way – other than by giving their children the deposit – is to act as a guarantor.

Most guarantor mortgages ignore the borrower's income and require the guarantor to have sufficient income to cover the whole of the mortgage they are guaranteeing – as well as any mortgage they already have. This is subject to the lender's normal income multiples. This means that many parents have insufficient income to allow them to act as guarantors.

Now the mortgage industry has taken note. One mortgage on the market treats the mortgage as a joint mortgage between parent and child enabling the child to borrow far more than with a guarantor mortgage because the parent's income is also taken into account. So if the parents have an income after their mortgage and other borrowing commitments of £25,000 and so does the child then the mortgage could be 2.75 x £50,000 = £137,500 – a far higher loan than if just one income was taken into account.

Another new mortgage offers the guarantor mortgage for professionals and graduates where the guarantor only needs enough income to cover that part of the mortgage which the borrower's income does not cover.

Whatever solution parents and children opt for, they should be aware of the commitment that is being made.

It is a legal requirement that everyone on the property deeds must always be on any mortgage deed – however, the reverse is not true. You can be on the mortgage deed but not on the property deed.

From a tax point of view parents may be advised not to be joint owners of the property – there can be capital gains tax implications as well as inheritance tax issues. However, lenders may prefer the guarantor to be on the deeds as it is easier for them to exercise their rights if the parent is on the deeds and the mortgage falls into arrears.

How much can you afford to borrow?

Even if a lender is prepared to advance you a large mortgage, remember that you must also take into account affordability. Interest rates can rise. In the late 1980s interest rates topped 15 per cent, millions of home buyers struggled to meet their repayments and tens of thousands had their homes repossessed. Check you would still be able to afford your mortgage if interest rates rose by a few per cent (see Appendix).

The alternative is to opt for a fixed or capped rate mortgage (these are explained later in this chapter), which will limit the maximum interest rate you will have to pay.

Lenders will often look at all your outgoings before deciding whether or not you can afford your mortgage repayments. Generally your monthly repayments should not exceed one third of your take-home pay. That way, if mortgage rates rise you will still be able to afford your repayments.

Your lender may ask you to fill in a questionnaire asking what your other outgoings are each month to make sure that you can afford to meet your monthly mortgage payments. You can work this out for yourself. Add up your monthly outgoings (if you don't have final figures use rough approximations):

■ monthly mortgage repayments plus life insurance/mortgage payment protection premiums;

■ service charges and ground rent (if you are buying a leasehold property);

■ insurance;

■ interest on other loans and credit cards;

■ gas/electricity/telephone bill;

■ travel/motoring costs;

■ food, clothes, entertainment;

■ and any other commitments, such as maintenance payments.

Now, then deduct those from your monthly after-tax income. You should find that you can easily afford to meet all these costs. Be realistic when estimating your outgoings and remember that once you buy a property it tends to be a drain on your finances. You will have to pay for furniture, renovations, repairs, maintenance and decoration.

Affordability varies in line with house prices and mortgage rates. At the height of the property market boom, the average buyer paid more than a quarter of their income in mortgage costs. That is now down to just over 15 per cent

Helping to finance your mortgage

For many first-time buyers paying monthly mortgage repayments is a struggle. Although you may qualify for a certain size of home loan and meet the affordability criteria, once you move into your property you will find that the extra costs can soar. But there are ways to help you meet these.

Cashbacks

A few lenders offer 'cashbacks', usually amounting to a few hundred pounds as an incentive for borrowers to take out a particular mortgage. These are explained in the section covering different types of mortgages. These cashbacks can help you through those first few expensive months when you move into a property.

Renting out a room

If you tell your lender that you intend to finance your mortgage by taking in a lodger or renting out part of the property, the lender is likely to think twice about advancing you such a large home loan. However, there is nothing to stop you taking in a lodger and under the Rent-A-Room scheme this rent can be *tax free.*

Most mortgage contracts require that borrowers seek permission from the lender before renting out a property. This is to ensure that you don't end up with a sitting tenant, as this will affect the value and saleability of the property. However, lodgers are usually exempt from this requirement. This is because they have no security of tenure (no rights).

In the current tax year you can earn £4,250 a year in rent tax free provided:

■ you rent out only one room in your property;

■ that room is furnished;

■ you don't rent out the room as a business (you are not running a B&B or guest house).

If you earn more than this allowance you can either:

■ earn the first £4,250 a year tax free and then pay tax on the amount of rent over this limit (at your top rate of tax); or

■ pay tax on your profits – rent minus expenses.

Generally if your expenses are less than £4,250 a year you will be better off claiming the Rent-A-Room allowance. Expenses can include a proportion of: the mortgage, insurance, gas, electricity and cleaning. If you have four rooms in your home and rent out one, you can generally claim a quarter of these costs. In addition you can deduct as an expense roughly 10 per cent of the rent to cover wear and tear of furnishings and the costs of advertising for a lodger.

Another alternative is to buy a property but not move into it for the first year. Rental incomes are currently running at between 6 and 10 per cent, so you should find that the rental covers the entire mortgage and earns you a small profit. At the same time you can hope to make a capital appreciation on the property. When your finances are less stretched you can then move into the property. Remember, you will have to earn enough in rent to cover the mortgage easily, you must ensure that the property is let with the agreement of your lender on an assured shorthold tenancy and you must be prepared to have weeks or months when you do not have a tenant/are advertising for a new tenant and will have to pay your mortgage and for renting alternative accommodation elsewhere.

How much can you borrow against the value of a property?

In addition to the size of mortgage a lender will advance as a multiple of your salary, the loan-to-value ratio will also affect the amount you can borrow. The ratio is the size of the mortgage in relation to the value of the property.

Generally, you will be required to pay at least a 5 per cent deposit. Although some lenders do offer 100 per cent home loans (and even up to 105 per cent) these are usually more expensive – interest rates can be higher and you may have to pay a high borrowing premium (see mortgage indemnity insurance).

To qualify for the cheapest home loans, you generally need to have a deposit of around 25 per cent.

Graduate mortgages

A few lenders will offer more than 100 per cent to graduates or professionals. These loans can be up to 105 per cent of the property value to cover expenses such as stamp duty and legal fees.

Mortgage indemnity

This is an extra cost that many homebuyers forget to budget for. It is an insurance charge that is paid by the borrower to protect the lender against losses should the buyer fall into arrears. Remember, although you as the buyer must pay the premium it protects the lender – not you. And if you are repossessed and the home is sold for less than the outstanding debt you could still be pursued for the losses, even though you have paid for the lender to have insurance against these losses.

The premium must generally be paid by those taking out a home loan for more than 75 to 90 per cent of the property value.

Most major lenders, like the Halifax, now require a much higher loan-to-value ratio – in other words a smaller deposit – before charging mortgage indemnity. The standard is now 90 per cent. Mortgage indemnity is charged on a sliding scale and can rise to 10 per cent of the outstanding loan on a 100 per cent mortgage. But it is only paid on the proportion above 75 per cent (in a few cases this can vary).

So if you are buying a £100,000 property with no deposit the costs could be as much as 10 per cent of £25,000 (25 per cent of the mortgage) or £2,500. For 85 per cent mortgages the rate falls to about 7 per cent. But rates charged do vary.

On a £60,000 mortgage you can pay between £500 and £1,400 in mortgage indemnity insurance if you have only a 5 per cent deposit.

To help borrowers meet the costs, lenders often allow the premium to be added to the outstanding mortgage loan. The snag with this is that the borrower will end up paying interest on it for 25 years. So if you can find an alternative way to finance it do your sums and you may find that over the longer run it is cheaper to pay for it in cash or to fund it using a low-rate shorter-term loan.

Some lenders allow homebuyers to pay the mortgage indemnity in 36 monthly instalments at the start of the loan. These extra payments should be taken into account when budgeting.

Warning: Not all lenders call their extra charge mortgage indemnity insurance. Some call it a high lending fee and others a scheme for maximum advances. So you may not realize what you are paying for or the fact that it provides you with no protection at all.

£ CASH TIP £

An increasing number of lenders no longer charge mortgage indemnity insurance. But this should not influence your mortgage choice entirely – weigh up the overall costs.

£ CASH TIP £

You cannot shop around for the best mortgage indemnity deal as you must purchase the one arranged by your lender. But you should compare the premiums charged by different lenders as premiums do vary. Some first-time buyer mortgages do not charge a mortgage indemnity premium (MIP).

£ CASH TIP £

The larger the deposit, the cheaper the mortgage indemnity. Some lenders will still charge mortgage indemnity insurance if you have a deposit of 25 per cent or less. Find out what rates are charged on different sizes of loan. By putting down a slightly larger deposit you may be able to save hundreds of pounds.

For instance, if you are buying a £50,000 property with a £2,500 deposit and mortgage indemnity is charged at 7.25 per cent on loans greater than 75 per cent of loan-to-value you would pay:

£47,500 (£50,000 purchase price – £2,500 deposit) –
£37,500 (75% of the loan to value) = £10,000
7.25% mortgage indemnity × £10,000 = £725

If you put down a further £100 deposit to bring the loan-to-value down to under 95 per cent and the mortgage indemnity rate fell to 6 per cent you would pay:

£47,400 (£50,000 – £2,600 deposit) – £37,500 (75% of
loan-to-value) = £9,900
6% mortgage indemnity × £9,900 = £594

So an additional £100 deposit will save you £131 in mortgage
indemnity premiums. Although few cases will be this clear-cut,
this gives an example of the savings that could be made.

> **Warning:** Most insurers have agreed with lenders that they
> can pursue the borrower for any shortfall – if the property is
> repossessed and sold for less than the amount of the
> outstanding mortgage and arrears. Some lenders have now
> stated that they will not chase evicted homebuyers for these
> debts. But it can still happen, even if the lender can recoup
> all or most of the losses from the mortgage indemnity
> insurance. So even after you have been repossessed and
> your property sold on – often for a fraction of the price you
> could have obtained – you may still be liable for the
> outstanding debt.

What if I don't have a deposit?

As already discussed, you will generally need a 5 per cent deposit.
So if you are buying a £50,000 property, you will need to have
£2,500 as a deposit. Remember that in addition to this deposit you
will also have to fund legal/conveyancing costs, stamp duty,
removal costs, insurance and possibly a mortgage arrangement
fee.

However, if – once you have budgeted for these extras – you
find that you do not have a sufficient deposit there are ways to get
round this problem:

- 100 per cent home loans – a few lenders offer these, as do
  some housebuilders. You may have to pay a higher interest

rate and your mortgage indemnity premiums will be high. Banks which currently offer 100 per cent loans include Bank of Scotland, Royal Bank of Scotland, Sainsbury's Bank and Scottish Widows.

▮ Borrowing the deposit – your lender will probably not be impressed if you say that you are borrowing the deposit. However, if you can persuade your parents to lend you the cash on an informal basis this will get round this problem. If you take out a mortgage with a *cashback* you may be able to repay all or part of the loan almost immediately.

Buying with a friend/your partner

In some cases the only way you can afford to get onto the property ladder is to buy the property with your partner, spouse, a relative or a friend.

The advantage is that you can borrow more money – usually three times the main salary plus the other salary or two-and-a-half times the joint income – and can split the costs.

The disadvantages are that if you fall out or if one of you wishes to sell and the other does not want to move, you could find that one buyer cannot afford to buy out the other owner. You may then be forced to sell the property even if you don't want to move. Also, if the joint-purchaser fails to meet his or her monthly mortgage repayments you will be jointly liable for the debts.

The risks of things going wrong are high, particularly if you do not have a long-term commitment to your relationship or friendship. Even married couples face a high risk, with more than one in three marriages ending in divorce.

A straightforward repayment loan may be better than an interest-only mortgage in these cases as you will not be forced to sell the investment purchased to repay the mortgage (which could mean you suffer if share prices are low) and it is easier to work out how much has been paid and how much is owing.

Types of joint ownership

If you are buying a property with another person you have two choices:

- joint tenancy; or

- tenancy in common.

Joint tenancies are the most common. Each person is assumed to own half the equity and if one partner dies the other inherits that person's share of the property, irrespective of what their will says.

Tenancy in common, the legal alternative, allows for varying financial arrangements. If you draw up a trust deed you can set down exactly how much each person has invested in the home. So if one partner has paid a bigger share of the deposit or pays more towards the mortgage, the deed enables the buyers to agree at the outset what will happen to the property should the relationship break down. Tenancy in common allows each of the owners to leave their share of the property in their will as they wish.

What if I can't find an affordable property?

Shared ownership

For those who cannot afford to buy a home but who still want to get onto the property ladder, shared ownership is an option. Under these schemes you part-rent and part-buy. Most of these schemes are run by housing associations.

In London, the London Home Ownership Group is an umbrella body of 30 associations which offer 5,000 homes a year to those who cannot afford to buy outright. Buyers do not have to be housing association or council tenants. Prices start from £15,000 of the available share and the typical age group for applicants is between 25 and 35 years old. However, people of any age can apply and no preference is given to younger people.

These schemes can help those who cannot save up the 10 per cent deposit usually required. The homebuyer buys a minimum of 25 per cent of the property with a mortgage and pays rent on the remainder. As his or her income rises or more capital is raised, further tranches of equity can be bought until the buyer owns 100 per cent of the property. These extra 'shares' of the property are then revalued by an independent surveyor.

Warning: Buyers can usually buy the remaining shares in the property in a maximum of four tranches. But as the price depends on the market value these extra tranches can cost far more than the first. So buyers may find that as prices continue to rise, they can never afford to buy the whole of the property.

The rent will not normally include insurance, repairs and maintenance. If you buy and rent with a 50/50 split the costs usually work out 30 per cent cheaper than buying outright.

Some lenders are reluctant to lend on this basis because the homebuyer does not own the entire property and therefore there is less security. However, some associations do underwrite any mortgage arrears.

Often the association has the right to find a suitable buyer at market value should the tenant want to sell. If no buyer is found within three months, then the owner has the right to sell the property on the open market.

Contacts: The Housing Corporation (020 7393 2000).

Part-ownership

Some developers have in the past offered homebuyers the option of buying 75 per cent of the property now and the remaining 25 per cent at a later date. The advantage is that initially you only have to pay three-quarters of the mortgage you would have paid on a comparable property.

However, after five years (this is the usual term) when you have to pay for the additional 25 per cent of the property you could find that you cannot afford it. Developers usually make you pay the market price and if the property market has boomed you could find that the 25 per cent share costs almost double what it would have originally cost. However, if the market has done well you should be able to sell the property reasonably easily and repay the remaining 25 per cent share out of the proceeds of the sale.

The mortgage application

What information you will need to supply

You will need to provide:

- proof of income;
- details of other spending commitments such as outstanding loans;
- bank details;
- details of your current landlord (possibly)/amount of rent you are paying;
- details of your employment record.

The lender will then want to check with your employer that you:

- are employed on a permanent contract (and since when);
- earn the salary/overtime/bonuses that you claim.

You may be required to arrange life insurance at the same time as taking out your mortgage. For this you will need to fill in a questionnaire asking for details about your current and past state of health and any medical conditions. You may need to undergo a medical examination.

What information the lender will check

Before advancing a loan, the lender will want to know that you
are creditworthy. They will probably write to your employer/
landlord/bank and check with a credit reference agency to find
out:

- if you have any county court judgements against you for non-
  payment of debts;

- if you have other outstanding loans/credit;

- your payment history – if you manage your finances well or
  have run into difficulty with loan/credit repayments in the
  past. Checks will be made with a credit reference agency.

Choosing a mortgage

There are several things you must consider. The extra costs of
taking out a mortgage are often overlooked. The actual cost of
taking out a home loan can vary widely, even though on the
surface there seems to be no difference in mortgage rates or terms.
This is because interest can be charged in different ways,
mortgage indemnity premiums vary and you may have to
purchase extra products (mortgage repayment protection
insurance or buildings and contents insurance). Another hidden
'cost' is that investment performance on endowment investment
policies varies widely and as such one home loan could leave you
far better off than another. So the golden rule is: do not just
compare interest rates – look at the total costs and benefits of a
mortgage.

Different types of mortgage

Repayment mortgages

These are by far the most popular. Each month you pay interest on the amount outstanding and repay an element of your outstanding debt.

Pros:

▌ Safe – if you make all the payments your loan will be repaid at the end of the mortgage term.

▌ If you switch mortgages you don't have to worry about taking out an extra endowment investment policy to cover a larger mortgage, although you may have to take out additional life insurance to cover the extra loan.

▌ They are much easier to understand and select. With interest-only mortgages you have to compare interest costs and select the best performing repayment vehicle. With repayments you need only pick the best rate.

▌ If you have a flexible/all-in-one mortgage, you can borrow back any amount of the mortgage you have repaid at the low mortgage rate. So if you have reduced your mortgage by £10,000, you can – for example – borrow £5,000 (increasing your mortgage) for home improvements.

Cons:

▌ At the end of the mortgage you have no lump sum. Investment-backed interest-only mortgages aim to repay the loan and may produce an extra cash payment.

Don't forget to add in the costs of separate life assurance (term assurance) that should be taken out to pay off your loan if you die.

Interest-only mortgages

These are far less popular as investment markets are no longer producing high returns and borrowers are more aware of the risks of linking their mortgages to the performance of the stock market. With these the homebuyer only pays interest on the outstanding loan and usually contributes to an investment that should produce sufficient returns to pay off the loan at the end of the mortgage term. None of the outstanding debt is repaid until the end of the term or when you sell your property. Interest-only mortgages can be backed by endowments, personal pensions and Individual Savings Accounts (ISAs).

Pros:
■ If your investment performs well you may have more than enough to repay your outstanding mortgage and have an extra tax-free lump sum on top.

■ With good investment performance (and a flexible repayment investment) you could repay your loan early.

■ If you opt for no repayment vehicle, the costs are cheaper than for a repayment mortgage – but your debt will not reduce.

Cons:
■ You do not repay any of the outstanding debt, so if you want to sell your property you will still have to repay the same size mortgage that you borrowed at the outset.

■ The value of your investment/endowment may not be sufficient to repay your mortgage at the end of the term. If investment performance is poor you may have to increase your premiums to cover any potential shortfall.

> **Warning:** If you need to cash in your endowment policy early or get into financial difficulties and can no longer afford the premiums you could get only a fraction of your investment returned. Once you have taken out an endowment policy you must keep paying the premiums for the full 25 years to get the maximum returns.

Endowment mortgages

These are no longer sold by most of the major mortgage lenders because poor investment performance has left thousands of borrowers with endowments that will not repay their mortgage debts. If you are recommended to take out an endowment mortgage, think twice – the consensus is that stock market investments and mortgages should be kept separate.

ISA mortgages

These use Individual Savings Accounts as the investment vehicle to repay your mortgage. The advantages are that they are tax-free investments and much more flexible than endowments, so that if the fund performs well you can decrease or stop your payments or repay your mortgage early. The drawback of ISAs is that they are directly linked to the stock market and as such their value can rise as well as fall. Life insurance must be arranged separately.

Pension mortgages

Remember your pension is primarily there to provide an income for retirement. Although there are currently tax breaks on pensions which means you receive tax relief at your highest rate on contributions and a tax-free lump sum on retirement, these tax breaks may not be guaranteed by future governments. You usually need to arrange separate life insurance, although you can receive tax relief on some life insurance contributions if they are part of your personal pension.

Pros:

▌ Significant tax advantages.

Cons:

▌ You may have less money on which to retire and you will have used up this valuable tax break on a mortgage rather than your pension.

> **Warning:** Few financial experts now recommend linking your mortgage – and therefore your home – to the stock market. The consensus is to keep your investments and pensions separate from your mortgage.

Flexible and all-in-one mortgages

These are one of the most popular types of home loan. You do not have to pay a fixed amount each month for the life of the mortgage and can increase, decrease or temporarily stop payments to suit your circumstances. These loans appeal to the self-employed, those with variable earnings and those who expect to earn large bonuses which they want to use to pay off chunks of their mortgage.

Some flexible mortgages are linked to current accounts and work as a combined loan and current account. Flexible mortgages can also offer repayment breaks of up to six months. However, the rates may not be the lowest on the market.

Pros:

▌ You can overpay each month to reduce the size of your loan.

▌ You can also use bonuses or windfalls to reduce your mortgage.

▌ All your borrowings – including your overdraft – can be at the low mortgage rate.

▌ If you have a change of circumstances – for instance if you start a family – you can reduce payments and underpay (often for six months).

▌ Any savings in linked current or savings accounts effectively 'earn' the mortgage rate which is usually far higher than the rates paid on most savings accounts.

▌ Some lenders also allow repayment holidays.

▌ If you have paid off some of your mortgage you can then take a lump sum out of your mortgage account to fund another purchase – releasing the equity in your home.

Cons:

▌ You will not qualify for the cheapest mortgage deals or cash-back offers, but some lenders do offer incentive payments (of up to 3 per cent of the mortgage advance).

▌ In some cases the minimum overpayment must be £500 or £2,000, so you may not be able to overpay small amounts each month.

The popularity of flexible mortgages is growing because the advantages are so great. The biggest advantage is that you can pay off your mortgage early by as much as 10 or 15 years and save thousands of pounds and you can make all of your money work for you.

There are no penalties for paying off your mortgage quickly and no charges for overpayment. You can also take payment holidays when money is tight. Add to this the fact that interest is calculated daily rather than annually and the savings add up to thousands of pounds over your mortgage term.

Paying your mortgage off early is a particularly good idea in times of low inflation when your outstanding debt does not decrease due to rising inflation. By paying in as little as £5 a week extra you can cut your mortgage term and save thousands.

However, the greatest benefits can come from combining all your finances into one account (all-in-one accounts) or linking them (offsetting). These types of mortgages will benefit those with some savings or money in their current accounts (however small) and who have borrowings such as credit cards and loans that are costing them more than the low mortgage rate.

Any credit balances, including your salary paid into your current account, are used to reduce the outstanding mortgage. As this is calculated daily even a few pounds left in your current account will result in an interest saving. So any savings effectively 'earn' the mortgage rate – which is usually far higher than the low rates paid on savings accounts. As this interest is 'saved' not 'earned' it is tax free. Other borrowings including credit card and loan balances can be linked to the mortgage or combined with it in an offset facility and are charged at the low mortgage rate.

Warning: These mortgages are not for everyone. If you have no savings and do not plan to repay your mortgage early you may be better off opting for a lower rate mortgage (such as a discount rate) with some flexible features as you could make greater interest savings.

Table 6.1 The interest savings from combining your finances and repaying your mortgage more quickly

	Interest savings	Time savings
Paying in £1,800 after-tax salary into £100,000 mortgage account	£3,073	pay off mortgage 5 months early
Paying in salary and leaving £20 a month in the account to reduce mortgage	£8,461	1 year, 11 months
Paying in salary and leaving £100 a month to reduce mortgage	£23,714	6 years, 5 months

Assumes a 25-year £100,000 mortgage on a £120,000 property. That net monthly income of £1,800 is paid into the account at the start of the month. That any overpayments are left in the account. Interest rate of 5.15%.
Source: One Account

Variable, fixed, capped or discount?

Discounted, capped and fixed-rate mortgages become more popular when interest rates are on the increase as borrowers try to protect their pockets by opting for lower initial rates or the security of a fixed or capped rate. However, because lenders can show the initial APR (the annual percentage rate of interest which reflects the true cost of borrowing) these can be difficult to compare. Always look at the cost of borrowing over the longer term – not just the first year or so. And watch out for redemption penalties if you switch or cash in your mortgage, as in some cases you will have to pay a financial penalty of six months' or more interest.

The proportion of fixed – as opposed to variable – rate mortgages is low in the United Kingdom compared to many European countries and the United States and is a source of concern for the government as fluctuations in interest rates cause economic problems. When interest rates are low there is a tendency for consumer credit to rocket and when rates rise UK households suffer far more than if they had a fixed-rate mortgage to provide them with financial certainty.

The Chancellor recently asked for a review of the situation – with a view to encouraging a greater uptake of long-term fixed-rate mortgages. The review by Professor David Miles had only reached interim conclusions at the time of writing. These included the tendency of borrowers to attach much greater weight to the level of initial monthly repayments than the overall cost of borrowing over the life of the loan. Borrowers should bear this in mind. However, as many borrowers switch mortgages every few years they are right to look for short-term savings.

Other interim findings include that many borrowers have a poor understanding of risk and therefore pay little attention to the insurance which longer-term fixed-rate mortgages can provide against unexpected interest rate rises. This is a valid point and borrowers should always understand that they may struggle to repay their mortgage should interest rates rise, and make contingency plans to cope – either by ensuring they are not overextended or setting aside savings.

One drawback of longer-term fixed rates – should the government push for their introduction – is that they tend to cost more than the low-cost short-term deals on offer – mainly discounted rate mortgages. As such they will appear more expensive.

Variable rate mortgages

The rate of most standard mortgages varies in line with interest rate moves. So you gain if rates fall, but must bear the brunt of any interest rate rises. See annually adjusted mortgages below.

Pros:
▌ More flexible, as you can usually cash in your mortgage without financial penalties.

Cons:
▌ If rates rise significantly you could find it difficult to meet your monthly mortgage payments.

> **Warning:** Some lenders take longer than others to pass on interest rate reductions and some increase rates more quickly when they rise. Over the term of a mortgage, the timing of rate moves can add considerably to the cost of your mortgage.

Tracker mortgages

Tracker mortgages guarantee that your mortgage rate will track the Bank of England base rate. So any cuts in interest rates will be passed on to you as the borrower. This should be the case with standard variable rate mortgages; however, lenders are not always very good at passing on full base rate cuts – to their credit, lenders don't always hike their rates to the full amount when interest rates rise either.

Annually adjusted mortgages

One-third of all mortgages have the monthly repayments adjusted annually – not when interest rates change. Although the amount of interest you are charged will change when interest rates rise and fall, your actual repayments do not. At the end of the year (usually in the spring) your monthly repayments will be adjusted to reflect any under- or overpayment of interest. When interest rates rise you may find that you are paying far less for your home loan than those with standard variable mortgages. However, when rates fall you are likely to pay more. Over the life-time of your mortgage you should not pay any more or less than with another type of home loan.

Pros:

▌ You know at the beginning of the year how much your monthly repayments will be.

Cons:

▌ If interest rates have risen significantly you could face a large increase in your monthly repayments once the annual adjustment takes place.

Fixed-rate mortgages

Fixed-rate mortgages are usually a safe option when interest rates are set to rise. However, you will find that rates are higher than for variable mortgages if lenders believe rate rises are likely.

The fixed rate usually applies for the first one to five years.

Pros:

▌ You know how much you will have to pay for the term of the fixed rate and if rates rise you will pay less than those with variable mortgages.

Cons:

▌ If rates are lower over the term of your fixed rate you will pay more interest than with a variable loan.

▌ When the fixed rate ends you can find that your monthly mortgage payments jump significantly.

▌ These loans are less flexible and if you cash in your mortgage in the first few years you could have to pay several months' interest as a penalty.

Warning: Once the fixed-rate period has finished you may be obliged to remain with the lender for a number of months or even a year or more or pay a financial penalty. So if the lender charges a higher-than-average rate you could lose out.

£ CASH TIP £

Do not take out a fixed-rate mortgage if you expect that interest rates will fall to below the level of the fix during the fixed-rate period – you will be locked in to paying a higher rate than most borrowers are paying.

£ CASH TIP £

Check that the loan is portable so that you can take it with you if you are moving up the property ladder. If it is not, and you need to cash in your mortgage, you will usually face financial penalties.

Warning: If you fall into arrears with a fixed-rate loan the penalties can be much higher than with other mortgages. So ask before taking out the mortgage.

Capped-rate mortgages

These are less common, but will appeal at a time of rising mortgage rates as they guarantee that rates will not rise above a set level or cap. In some cases they are 'collared', which means that a minimum rate of interest has also been set so any rate reductions below this level will not be passed on to the borrower. These are known as cap and collar mortgages. The capped rate can apply for anything from the first five years to the full term of the mortgage.

Pros:
▪ You know that for the period of the capped rate you will never pay more than a certain level of interest.

Cons:
▪ If you cash in your mortgage in the first few years you may have to pay financial penalties.

▪ If the mortgage also has a minimum interest rate you could find that if interest rates fall you will not get the benefit of very low mortgage rates.

Discount mortgages

These give you a discount of anything between 0.25 and 5 per cent off the variable rate of interest for the first few months or years of the mortgage. These are only usually offered to:

▪ first-time buyers;

▪ new borrowers (who are switching their mortgage from another lender).

Pros:
▪ For the term of the discount you will pay less than other borrowers.

Cons:

▮ Check what rate will apply after the discount period has ended as you may have to pay a higher rate than other borrowers.

▮ There are usually high penalties for all or part repayment of the loan in the first few years and borrowers may be required to repay all of the discount if they cash in their mortgage.

£ CASH TIP £

Check that the interest is discounted and not deferred. If it is deferred it will be added to the outstanding loan and you could end up with a larger mortgage than you started with.

Incentives

Tough competition between mortgage lenders means that many offer first-time and new borrowers inducements.

At time of print many mortgage companies are offering appealing incentives. For example, most offer first-time buyers no mortgage indemnity (MIP) or free accident, sickness and unemployment insurance for six months. Other incentives include free valuation fees or cashbacks which can be as much as 2 per cent of the amount advanced.

Free services

Some lenders offer to waive the valuation fee or pay for some of your legal costs.

The mortgage term

Although most mortgages are taken over a 25-year period or term there is nothing to stop you choosing a shorter or longer pay-back term from 10 to 30 years.

With a repayment mortgage, the shorter the term the higher the monthly costs.

With an interest-only loan, the length of the mortgage term makes no difference to the interest payments since the debt stays the same. However, you will have to invest more in either your endowment, PEP or pension plan to ensure that your investment is adequately funded to repay the loan at the end of a shorter mortgage term. So if you want a shorter-term mortgage, a repayment mortgage may be the better option.

If you cut a £100,000 mortgage term from 25 years to 15 years and pay interest at a rate of 6 per cent you will pay £41,200 less interest over the term of the mortgage for an extra monthly payment of £206 a month. The only problem is that if you are borrowing near the maximum allowed and rates increase you will probably find it hard to meet your monthly mortgage bill. However, as you will be repaying the capital much faster, if you have to move you will have greater equity in the property. Table 6.2 illustrates the effect of reducing the mortgage term on monthly repayments.

Table 6.2 How reducing the mortgage term increases monthly repayments

Term of loan	Monthly cost £100,000 mortgage
10 years	£1,132
15 years	£858
20 years	£727
25 years	£652

Assumes an interest rate of 6 per cent.
Source: The Council of Mortgage Lenders

Comparing the cost of different mortgages

Mortgages are no longer straightforward. Cashbacks, discounts, fixed rates and arrangement fees mean you will have to compare more than just the interest rates. These are the aspects of the mortgage you should compare:

Interest-only v repayment: Don't just compare the monthly payments. With a repayment mortgage you should add any life insurance premiums to the monthly costs and with an interest-only mortgage the endowment premiums or the costs of another type of repayment investment.

Interest rates and how interest is charged: Mortgages have been covered by 'annual percentage rate' rules since 1987. The APR should give the true cost of borrowing and include the cost of any mortgage indemnity guarantee, brokerage or arrangement fees, valuation costs, redemption penalties and compulsory insurances. However, because the APR can be given on the initial fixed or discount rate it makes the true cost over 25 years very difficult to compare.

The best way to compare costs is to add up 12-monthly repayments over 5 to 10 years (few borrowers stick with the same mortgage for 25 years). Take into account any discounts or short-term fixed rates.

Also, you will find that interest is charged in different ways. Most building societies take payments in advance, but bank mortgages are usually paid in arrears.

Homebuyers with *repayment mortgages* could be paying £73 billion in unnecessary interest charges on their mortgages over the next 25 years because not all lenders calculate interest in the same way, according to calculations from Yorkshire Bank.

In the past, most lenders calculated interest annually, basing the next 12 months' payments on the mortgage balance outstanding on the first day of the year. No account was made of payments credited to the repayment mortgage over the subsequent 12-month period. This cost borrowers some £160 million a year.

Increasingly lenders calculate interest daily, working out interest on the balance outstanding at the end of each day.

Redemption penalties: If you agree to pay redemption penalties (a charge if you cash your mortgage in within the first few years) you will usually be offered a lower mortgage rate. However, if you do need to move you could find that the savings of a fixed-rate or discount mortgage do not make up for the redemption costs.

Warning: Think twice before making additional mortgage payments as some loans do not allow even part repayments of the mortgage without triggering redemption penalties

---

£ CASH TIP £

In many cases lenders allow you to take your mortgage with you when you move. This way you avoid hefty redemption penalties often totalling up to several thousand pounds.

Arrangement fees: In some cases you may be charged an arrangement fee. Always ask in advance what this will be, and if it will be refunded should you be forced to pull out of a property purchase.

Tied products: In some cases you may be required to take out buildings and contents insurance arranged by the lender as a condition of the loan. If the insurance is much more expensive than you can arrange elsewhere you will lose out.

How to calculate the costs of different mortgages

You should add up how much the mortgage will cost you in total – not just the monthly repayments. As first-time buyers usually move up the property ladder after a few years, compare the costs in the first five years.

Do not forget to take into account extra costs in addition to the monthly mortgage repayments.

A two-year discount mortgage with a higher rate than a one-year discount mortgage can actually work out cheaper once you do the maths.

Arrangement fees, compulsory insurance (this can work out more expensive than shopping around for house insurance) and any redemption penalties should be included in your calculations. Remember also that after the low rate ends you will be charged the uncompetitive standard variable rate and if you are tied into this rate for six months or a year you could end up paying more for what looks like a cheap deal. Web sites such as www.charcolonline.co.uk enable you to compare the total costs, not just the monthly repayments.

Mortgage illustrations

When you approach a bank, building society, financial adviser or mortgage broker to discuss a mortgage you should be given a mortgage illustration. This will usually show:

- the amount of the loan (and the value of the property);

- the term of the loan (number of years);

- the number of monthly repayments;

- the interest rate;

- the monthly mortgage payments;

- the total gross amount payable over the term of the loan (and what this includes – life insurance/endowment premiums are usually in addition);

- the APR and what this includes such as
  - legal fees
  - valuation fees

- any arrangement/administration fees
- mortgage guarantee insurance/indemnity insurance fees
- remittance fees and any other costs;

▌ the amount and cost of term assurance to protect a repayment loan, or the endowment if you are taking out an endowment mortgage;

▌ the warnings 'YOUR HOME IS AT RISK IF YOU DO NOT KEEP UP REPAYMENTS ON A MORTGAGE OR OTHER LOANS SECURED ON IT' and 'Be sure you can afford the repayments before entering into a credit agreement';

▌ details of any other products you have to buy as a condition of the loan (for instance buildings insurance).

You should also be given an illustration of the costs of any insurance you take out to protect your mortgage repayments should you lose your job or become too ill to work. *Do not confuse mortgage protection plans for payment protection plans. The former is often used to describe term life assurance policies and does not protect repayments, only the outstanding loan in the event of death.*

Read the illustration carefully. If, for instance, there are extra fees – such as arrangement fees – included on the illustration, but you were not told earlier that you would have to pay them, do not assume they are listed in error.

The agreement in principle/mortgage certificate

If the lender agrees a loan they will often give you a certificate showing how much they are prepared to lend (subject to a valuation and structural survey of the property). It will state that this offer is only valid for a limited period. Often this is as little as six weeks, but it can be for up to three months.

As it may take you weeks or even months to find a property to suit your needs you may want to keep your mortgage options open.

If you have secured a particularly good deal on a mortgage you may be able to agree with the lender that the mortgage you want is held for a specific period of time. In this case you will have to sign a form accepting the mortgage offer. Then, once your offer on a particular property has been accepted, you can finalize the mortgage advance.

Protecting your mortgage repayments

Some 2.5 million of the 10 million homebuyers risk serious arrears on their mortgage payments if they become sick or unemployed. Cuts in social security mean it is now advisable to buy insurance that will cover your monthly repayments. Eighty per cent of borrowers receive no assistance with mortgage interest payments for the first nine months after stopping work.

It is usually easier and cheaper to take out this cover at the same time as your mortgage. You do not have to buy it from your mortgage lender but can shop around to find a lender that offers this insurance at a cheaper rate.

Lenders are now offering more than just mortgage protection insurance. Some offer a mix of life insurance, critical illness cover (which pays a lump sum if you suffer a specific medical condition such as a heart attack), permanent health insurance (which pays you an income for a set period of time if you can no longer work due to ill health or redundancy) and unemployment cover in one policy.

Since 1 July 1999, new standards in mortgage payment protection insurance (MPPI) have been in place. All policies must pay out after a maximum of 60 days – in the past policies have had excess periods of up to 120 days. But still watch out for the small print, check for exclusions and find out for how long payments will be made.

> **Warning:** Read the small print of your mortgage protection policy, especially if you are self-employed or a contract worker. If you are made redundant, you may not receive the full 12-month payout if your contract would have finished before the end of the 12 months. If you cannot work due to ill health, any past medical problems or periods of sickness may invalidate your policy if you do not declare these when you first take the policy out.

Mortgage tax relief

Note, tax relief is no longer given on mortgage interest.

For further information

Visit www.fsa.gov.uk for mortgage comparative tables and useful leaflets including *What to do when you can't meet your mortgage payments*.

The Council of Mortgage Lenders at www.cml.org.uk has useful consumer information and a mortgage calculator, as well as a guide to help and benefits if you cannot meet your mortgage repayments, a guide to the Mortgage Code and information on how to protect your mortgage repayments.

7 Preliminaries: costs appraisal and appointing a solicitor/conveyancer

Budgeting for the extra costs

If you are buying a house costing £100,000 you will need to find an average of £1,792 to cover your buying costs, according to the annual Woolwich Cost of Moving Survey. This figure includes £1,000 for stamp duty, just over £500 for your solicitor and £170 to cover Land Registry fees and searches. Note that this does not even include survey fees, removal vans, mortgage arrangement fees, the deposit or the cost of curtains, carpets and furniture. Typical removal costs are around £456 and average survey costs around £400.

Unsurprisingly, your deposit could be your biggest cost with the largest deposits made by first-time buyers in the high-priced areas of Greater London, the South East, the South West and East Anglia. An average first-time buyer in London now makes a deposit of over £41,000 (22 per cent of the property value) to buy their first home while a first-time buyer in the North currently puts down a deposit of £6,528 (12 per cent of property value).

So some first-time buyers may need to find as much as £45,000 to get onto the property ladder.

Be prepared for a potential purchase to fall through. Often you may have to pay for more than one survey and extra legal fees. Table 7.1 illustrates the typical costs of buying a home.

However, the risk of having to pay for surveys and legal costs on more than one property should be reduced when the new Home Information Pack (HIP, also known as the seller's pack) is introduced in 2006. This should speed up the buying process, reducing the risk of gazumping (when another purchaser comes along and offers a higher price, snatching the property from you) and the risk of finding problems with a property once a survey has been conducted. The HIP, which will be compulsory when it is introduced, will contain a home condition report based on a professional survey of the property. The government estimates that around 30 per cent of all property sales fall through each year at a cost of £350 million to consumers.

Stamp duty

This is a tax that has to be paid on property costing over £60,000 and is charged at 1 per cent of the total purchase price (not just the proportion above £60,000). It rises to 3 per cent on properties over £250,000 and 4 per cent above £500,000. So if you buy a property that is worth less than £60,000 you pay no stamp duty. But on a property worth £100,000 you will pay £1,000.

However, if you buy in a disadvantaged area (there are 2,000 council wards across the country) you will not need to pay stamp duty unless the property is worth £150,000 or more.

£ CASH TIP £

If you are buying a property valued just above one of these stamp duty bands you may be able to agree a purchase price below the band level and make up the difference by agreeing a separate figure for curtains, carpets and other fixtures and fittings. However, the Inland Revenue is wise to this so you cannot claim to be paying £1,000 – for example – for a light fitting.

Legal fees

Conveyancing fees vary. However, the charges may be more if the land is registered than if it is unregistered. The average conveyancing fee is about £500 for a £100,000 property. You may have to pay for extra services on top of the fees and VAT will be added. Always agree fees in advance. They tend to rise for homes worth more. The fees should include local authority searches and Land Registry fees.

These legal fees should fall dramatically in future once the HIP becomes compulsory from 2006 (if legislation is passed by then). The vendor will pay (around £600) for these packs which will include many of the legal checks that need to be made including:

▌ terms of sale;

▌ evidence of title;

▌ replies to standard searches;

▌ planning consents, agreements and directions and building control certificates;

▌ replies to standard preliminary enquiries made on behalf of buyers;

▌ copies of warranties and guarantees;

▌ for leasehold properties – a copy of the lease, most recent service charge accounts and receipts, building insurance policy details and payment receipts, regulations made by the landlord or management company and memorandum and articles of the landlord or management companies.

The HIP will be good news for first-time buyers who should find it cheaper to get onto the housing ladder as the seller will cover a number of the costs they have previously paid. Legal fees are already being reduced in anticipation.

The Halifax, for example, recently introduced a £300 'no sale, no fee' conveyancing package for properties below £100,000.

Survey costs

These vary from about £250 for a valuation report (a very basic survey) to around £400 for a homebuyer's survey and upwards of £400 for a full structural survey.

Once again these costs could fall once the HIP is introduced, as this will include a home condition report based on a professional survey of the property. However, purchasers of older homes will still be advised to pay for their own full structural survey.

Removal costs

As a first-time buyer you may have little furniture to move so the cheapest way will be to hire a van and do it yourself.

Mortgage indemnity guarantee (MIG)

As discussed earlier (pages 67–70), this can often add between £600 and £1,000 to the costs of buying a home – although many lenders offer MIG or MIP (mortgage indemnity premium) free loans for first-time buyers.

How the costs add up

Table 7.1   Typical cost of buying a home

Purchase price	£50,000	£100,000	£150,000	£200,000
Solicitor	£468	£522	£576	£637
Land Registry	£40	£100	£150	£150
Searches	£170	£170	£170	£170
Stamp Duty	0	£1,000	£1,500	£2,000
TOTAL*	£678	£1,792	£2,396	£2,957

*Note: this excludes removal costs, surveys, mortgage arrangement fees, the deposit and high lending fees. Costs vary around the country with costs highest in the South East.
Source: The Woolwich

Remember that VAT is added to legal/conveyancing fees. Also, you may be charged a bank transfer charge when the money is transferred using the CHAPS banking system.

Note that buying costs are not the only costs to budget for. You also need to budget for running costs. The costs of owning and running a house have risen nearly three times faster than the rate of inflation. The cost of actually owning the typical UK household is now £5,604 a year, according to the Halifax. Increases in council tax and water, gas and electricity bills pushed up the cost by 7.2 per cent in the year from 2001 to 2002.

Council tax alone accounts for nearly 14 per cent of the cost of owning and running a home. For more information, see Chapter 14.

Appointing a solicitor/conveyancer

Before you start to house-hunt, you should also decide on how you will handle your conveyancing and who will handle it for you. This is so that you can inform the estate agent of your solicitor's/conveyancer's details the moment you make an offer and it is accepted. This will speed up the buying process and reduce the risks of being gazumped by another buyer who offers a higher price for the property or who can exchange contracts more quickly.

Conveyancing is the legal act of transferring the right of ownership (the title of the property). It involves checking:

▮ that the vendor really owns the property;

▮ that there are no outstanding disputes regarding the property (such as planning disputes);

▮ if there are any covenants attached to the property and that these are not unduly restrictive;

▮ there are no undisclosed charges or mortgages against the property;

▮ there is no planning permission in the pipeline that will affect the property.

You don't have to employ a solicitor. There are three alternatives:

- employ a solicitor;
- employ a licensed conveyancer;
- do your own conveyancing.

Handling your own conveyancing

Deregulation of the market means that fees have dropped considerably so there is less of a saving if you handle conveyancing yourself.

Fees used to be set at around 1 per cent of the property value, but now can be as low as 0.2 per cent. As such the savings from doing it yourself are often only £300.

If you do handle your own conveyancing your lender is likely to employ its own solicitor to double check your work. You will then have to pay for this. As such the savings are likely to be less than £100 and because of the work/time involved you may find that you lose out on a purchase as a result.

Choosing a solicitor/conveyancer

Deregulation of the market means you now have a choice of a solicitor or licensed conveyancer to handle the mechanics of buying your home. A local firm will be better as it will be aware of any local planning applications and even problems with leases or local landlords. As with all aspects of the homebuying process, it pays to shop around.

Often a firm of local estate agents or your lender may be able to recommend a firm of solicitors.

Always agree conveyancing fees in advance. Ask for a written quotation of costs. Remember VAT will be added and there will usually be extras. Ask for a good indication of what these could add up to before employing a solicitor.

Also check that the solicitor can handle the conveyancing quickly and efficiently. You don't want to lose a property because the legal work has delayed the buying process.

The Home Information Pack

Widely known as the seller's pack, the Home Information Pack (HIP) will be introduced in 2006 (provided legislation is passed) and will change the way homes are bought. Much of the legal work will be included in these packs (which are covered in detail in Chapter 9). However, you will still need to appoint a solicitor or conveyancer. The changes should mean that there will be competitive fixed-rate conveyancing deals on offer from a range of providers including mortgage lenders and estate agents.

8 House-hunting

Location

It may sound like a cliché that estate agents say the three most important factors when choosing a property are 'location, location, location', but it *is* true.

Although house price surveys give a headline figure for house price growth, when it comes to different areas – and even different streets – there are often marked differences in price rises, with some areas barely seeing prices rise at all and others seeing increases of 10 or 20 per cent.

At the same time, more popular areas suffer less when prices fall. During the slump from the late 1980s to mid-1990s in parts of London's Docklands, property values slumped by up to 50 per cent. Yet in the more established and desirable areas of the capital, such as Chelsea, prices hardly suffered at all.

Although your main priority may be space or a garden, estate agents generally recommend a 'rabbit hutch' in a good location over a larger property in a less desirable area.

Making money may not be your priority, but remember, as a first-time buyer you are only taking your first step onto the property ladder. You will probably want to move again in the next few years and by buying a property in a more desirable area you will find it easier to get a buyer and should make more of a profit to help you trade up to a bigger home.

Where you buy also has a big impact on the quality of your life and how much it costs to live in the property.

Postcodes not only affect the value of your property but also:

■ the cost of insurance – not just buildings and contents but also motor insurance;

■ council tax;

■ where your children can go to school (there is always good demand for properties near schools that appear at the top of school league tables). If you have a family or are planning one, check the property falls into the right catchment area;

■ and in London in particular, whether or not you can get a parking permit for a particular borough in central London.

Prices on different sides of the same street can differ by as much as 10 or 20 per cent as a result. Remember, subtle boundaries such as postcodes often differentiate what is a desirable area and what is not.

In London you can get 15 to 20 per cent more if you are within 10 minutes' walk of an underground station. In central London houses and flats with garaging or off-street parking also carry a premium of at least 10 per cent.

Houses with gardens, or near gardens, parks and good schools, are always in demand.

Spotting the right location

You are probably already aware of the most desirable streets in your area. The ones where the properties look well maintained, that are near to facilities and yet quiet, always command higher prices than similar properties in less sought after locations.

These areas are likely to be out of your price bracket as a first-time buyer. However, as an alternative you can buy:

■ on the fringes of the most desirable areas;

■ in up-and-coming areas (however, this often means that until recently the area was a no-go area for homebuyers and you are taking a chance that it will improve).

How to spot an up-and-coming area

These are the areas that estate agents believe will increase in value and popularity in the years ahead. However, as the name implies, they are not yet established as desirable and there is no guarantee that they will. Some cynics say estate agents use the phrase to make an undesirable area seem more attractive.

Up-and-coming areas are those which are going to benefit from better transport links – a new tube line, better railway service or new road links. And those where new employers are moving into the area, creating jobs and prosperity.

In urban areas, those that are near to the centre but have yet to become fashionable are also worth looking at. An up-and-coming area is easy to spot by the number of developments by property companies building new homes or converting offices/wharfs. A large number of skips as homeowners renovate rundown older properties is also a good sign.

Setting your priorities

Most homebuyers rely on gut instinct rather than rational reasons when buying a home.

Location remains the most important factor for four out of five homebuyers and nearly 80 per cent decide to buy a home within a matter of seconds after walking through the front door. To stop yourself from making a rash decision based on appearances alone, you should make a list of your priorities.

These will vary from buyer to buyer depending on needs and taste. However, after price the following are likely to be priorities:

- near good quality transport links;

- good local amenities such as late-night shops, supermarkets, cinemas, bars and restaurants, and if you have children, good schools;

▋ enough space – many first-time buyers prefer an extra room so they can rent it out if they are strapped for cash;

▋ style of property – either a flat in a Victorian conversion or a modern, hassle-free home;

▋ car parking – either in a garage or easy street parking;

▋ similar people to yourself – you may not enjoy living in an area full of retired couples and will probably have more fun in an area favoured by young first- and second-time buyers;

▋ security – as you will be out at work all day your home is more at risk of being burgled. Don't pick a property next to a crime-ridden council estate and check there is good street lighting and adequate security features on the property;

▋ garden, patio or balcony;

▋ near or overlooking a park or other open space or water;

▋ low running/maintenance costs.

Remember, it is unlikely that you will find a property that meets all of these criteria. Six out of ten is normally the compromise you will have to reach.

What each of us looks for in a property

As with most things in life, there is a difference in the sexes: men tend to look at size and price and women at finish and ambience. Estate agents find that it is easier to sell to men as they tend not to look at the practicalities. So if you are a man bear that in mind. Women, on the other hand, are less likely to take a reduction in the asking price – so bear that in mind if you are buying from a woman.

So, although you have made a list of your priorities, when viewing a property this is what will – according to one recent survey – actually sway your mind:

Men:

Square footage	Price
Address	Shower
High ceilings	Unusual properties with
Room for big sofas	exposed brick or gadgets
Large reception room with	Big hallway (for golf clubs,
fireplace	skis, etc)

Women:

Crisp and clean	Good security
A garden	Plenty of good quality
Dressing room	cupboards
Practical layout	Sunlight and views
Dining area	Well-equipped kitchen
Ambience and location	Comfort

Different types of property

The chances are that you are simply looking for a flat or a starter home you can afford in a suitable area.

But you may also have a set idea of the type of property you want to buy. You may want a light airy flat in a converted period property, or a modern starter home that is fully fitted and easy to maintain.

The property may be leasehold or freehold. It could be old, modern or newly built. It may be fully modernized or need extensive work. The type of property you want to buy will affect the buying process and, once you move in, the running costs.

There has been a fundamental shift in housing demand due to the growth in the number of single people buying houses, as well as the growing trend towards apartment-style living.

Terraced houses and flats are the most popular purchases for first-time buyers. In 1983, most opted for either a terraced or a semi-detached property when buying their first home. The trend has now changed and first-time buyers are favouring terraced houses and flats and maisonettes over all other property types.

Leasehold or freehold

These are the two main types of property ownership: leasehold and freehold.

Leasehold

Generally, if you are buying a flat or, in some cases, a house on an estate you will become a leaseholder. When you buy a leasehold property you purchase a lease for a set number of years – from as little as 10 to as many as 999.

Once the term of the lease has finished, you no longer own the property. As a result, properties with shorter leases are worth less than those with longer ones. Most mortgage lenders will not advance mortgages on properties that have leases with less than 50 years to run as, when the lease starts to run out, these properties can be difficult to resell.

If you buy a leasehold property you will have to pay:

▌ ground rent;

▌ service charges.

Ground rents are usually low, but you should ask your solicitor to check if they can be increased in future. There have been horror stories of leaseholders threatened with rent rises from £120 to £4,160 a year. In some cases, leaseholders may be offered the chance to buy the freehold of their property (see **Leasehold Reform** on page 113).

Service charges

Service charges can easily add up to over £100 a month on flats and can rise sharply. The service charge usually includes: buildings insurance, maintenance of the building, cleaning and lighting of communal areas and a 'sinking fund' to pay for major repairs such as a new roof or repainting.

£ CASH TIP £

Check if any major repairs are planned on a leasehold property as you may find that the seller wants to move out before having to chip in several thousand pounds to pay for these. Also, check if service charges are due to rise, how often they rise, if there is a 'sinking fund' to cover major repairs and if other leaseholders are happy with the quality of management.

Commonhold

This new type of home ownership was introduced following the commencement of the Commonhold and Leasehold Reform Act in May 2002. In future there are likely to be commonhold developments built to take advantage of the new law.

Commonhold enables a group of people to own the component freehold parts of a property and gives them the right to manage it. In effect it is equivalent to owning a freehold flat (something that was not possible before).

An alternative may be when a group of leaseholders buy the freehold under the leasehold enfranchisement law and they become leaseholders who also own a share of the freehold. They can therefore determine the length of their lease and other matters such as the amount of service charges levied and any repairs that need to be undertaken.

In a commonhold development each separate property will be known as a unit and the owner a unit-holder. The body that owns and manages the common parts will be known as the Commonhold Association.

A commonhold can be created where there is a freehold or where all the leasehold tenants agree to form a commonhold. The situation where there is a lease and commonhold on the same property cannot exist.

The Commonhold Association will be a company limited by guarantee and all the unit-holders will have a direct interest in the unit they own and an interest in the Commonhold Association that owns the common parts.

The main advantage of a commonhold property is that the buyer will own the property indefinitely, whereas a lease diminishes year by year.

However, there are extra responsibilities for each commonholder who will generally be involved in the running of the building – if only to vote on matters such as service charges or maintenance.

The Commonhold Association will have to lodge documents including the Certificate of Incorporation, the Memorandum and Articles of Association and the Commonhold Community Statement at the Land Registry. This statement sets out the detailed management structure covering the rights and duties of the association and the unit-holders. Issues such as insurance, repairs and maintenance of the individual unit(s) must be disclosed, and the rights to be granted over each unit must be disclosed and these rights can vary from unit to unit dependent on design, construction and use. Service charge apportionment must also be disclosed.

The sale of part of the commonhold unit can only take place with the agreement of 75 per cent of the Commonhold Association.

Leasehold issues

> **Warning:** If you fail to pay your service charges your property can be repossessed, even if you have managed to keep up-to-date on your mortgage repayments.

> **Warning:** When you move into a leasehold property check that the previous owner is up-to-date on all service charge and ground rent payments.

Warning: There have been horror stories about unscrupulous landlords charging leaseholders exorbitant service charges to cover maintenance and repairs. The freeholder can also make life difficult by deciding to build an extra flat on the roof or extend the property, by failing to maintain the property adequately or by trying to force leaseholders to move out so that the property can be redeveloped. It is advisable to ask other leaseholders (not just the vendor) about the freeholder and management company.

The lease will also have restrictions placed on the use of the property. For instance:

■ a requirement that you must redecorate every three or five years;

■ a restriction on noise after 11pm;

■ a requirement to dispose of rubbish on a certain date or in a certain way;

■ a ban on pets;

■ a restriction on what you can use the property for.

Dealing with problems

If you are in dispute with your landlord over high service charge bills, poor management or shoddy repairs you can take your case to the new network of eight Leasehold Valuation Tribunals (LVTs).

The tribunals have the power to settle disputes over service charges and insurance, to look into disagreements over proposed building works and – if the tribunals decide the existing management is unsatisfactory – to appoint new managers to run blocks of flats. The decisions of the tribunals are legally enforceable, although there is an appeals procedure. The tribunals will deal with disputes for a fixed fee. The role of these tribunals was strengthened under the Commonhold and Leasehold Reform Act to make them more effective and efficient. The right to seek the appointment of a new manager by the LVT was strengthened and leaseholders now have more rights against unreasonable charges levied under their lease and have greater rights to be consulted about service charges. Charges levied by landlords under Estate Management Schemes can now be challenged before a LVT and the accounting rules for lease-holders' monies have been strengthened. Landlords must also now hold service charge funds in designated separate client accounts.

Leaseholders can apply for a determination of reasonableness of charges for services, repairs, maintenance, insurance or management – including costs that have already been incurred. If there are severe problems with the management of their building they can then apply to the LVT for the removal of the manager and the appointment of a new one.

LVTs are independent and impartial. They normally consist of three members: a lawyer, a valuer and a layperson. Hearings are semi-formal and evidence is not given on oath. The tribunal provides a quicker and simpler option to court proceedings.

Applicants do not have to be represented by a solicitor or barrister, although professional assistance is recommended. The tribunal will hear both sides of the argument and then determine the issue. Their determination is issued in writing a short time after the hearing.

Applicants who choose not to be legally represented will be responsible for putting their case in front of the tribunal. They will have to present arguments and evidence to support their own case. Applicants cannot expect tribunal members to assist them in this, as the latter are independent. It is important that evidence should be presented clearly and concisely and should be confined to the matters in the dispute.

So while disputes may continue, there are now fewer risks in buying a leasehold property following the introduction of the Commonhold and Leasehold Reform Act because leaseholders now have more rights, including the right to manage their property – provided certain criteria are met.

Right to manage: This allows leaseholders the right to take over the management of their building, reflecting the fact that it is more often the case that leaseholders have the greatest financial interest in the building. Right to manage is an alternative to the right to enfranchisement (the right to buy the freehold), and will, for example, allow leaseholders the opportunity of managing the building before committing to buying the freehold; if managing the building proves successful, then the leaseholders can buy the freehold under the right to enfranchisement.

Leaseholders will be able to take over the management of their building without having to prove fault on the part of the landlord or pay him or her any compensation.

To prevent minorities from taking control of the management of buildings, at least half the flats must be on leases with two-thirds of the flats on long leases and three-quarters of the building must be residential.

Leaseholders who exercise the right to manage will need to incorporate a company limited by guarantee.

Short-lease properties

If you are looking for a central London location the only property you may be able to afford is a short-leasehold property. Provided these are enfranchisable under the 1993 Leasehold Reform Act they can be good value, but you must be prepared for a long battle if you want to buy the freehold.

Mortgage lenders are unlikely to lend on a property with a lease of less than 50 or 60 years. As a result, short leaseholds tend to be far cheaper than freeholds or properties with longer leases. So you will need either a substantial deposit or to be able to afford to buy the property outright as you may not be able to get a mortgage.

Short leaseholds (as with freeholds) are usually fully repairing, which means that if the property is in poor condition you could find yourself with a huge bill for dilapidations. Or else you may face crippling service charges.

Leasehold reform

If you buy a leasehold property you now have more protection and rights under the Commonhold and Leasehold Reform Act, which became law in 2002.

You may be able to:

▌ extend your lease;

▌ buy a share of the freehold.

Leaseholders have for some time been able to buy their freehold and extend their leases but a number of the criteria have now been removed (for example, the requirement to prove residence in the flat) and as such more leaseholders will benefit from these rights.

Extending the lease: The right for long leaseholders of flats to acquire a new 90-year lease after the expiry of their existing leases on payment of a premium is an individual right. It provides a useful alternative to the right of buying the freehold (collective enfranchisement) in cases where, for example, there are insufficient qualifying tenants in the block or there is insufficient support.

Under the new Act leaseholders must own a long lease (one, which when originally granted, was for a term exceeding 21 years). They must also have owned the lease for a period of two years before being able to exercise the right and must not have sublet the flat on a long lease.

It is unlikely that as a first-time buyer you will be buying a flat with a lease that is about to expire (as you will not be able to get a mortgage). However, this right is worth knowing about as you may be able to extend a lease that is reducing (for example, one with 80 years to run) to protect the value of the property.

Following the changes made by the Commonhold and Leasehold Reform Act 2002 the price payable is:

▌ the reduction in the value of the landlords' interests in the flat as a result of the granting of the new, longer lease plus half *of any marriage value* (marriage value will only be payable on leases with less than 80 years left to run and is the extra value added to the property as a result of the longer lease); and

■ compensation (where relevant) for severance or other losses resulting from the granting of a new, longer lease (for example, loss of development value).

Further Information

The Office of the Deputy Prime Minister – www.odpm.gov.uk – has several useful publications. Search under *Housing* and then *Guidance for Homeowners, Tenants and Landlords* and look under *Publications* for *Booklets for homeowners on long leaseholds*.

These include:

■ *Your right to buy the freehold of your building or renew your lease*

■ *Applying to a Leasehold Valuation Tribunal*

■ *Lease running out? Security of tenure for long leaseholders.*

Freehold

If you buy a house this will generally be on a freehold basis. This means that you have bought the absolute ownership of the property and the land on which it stands.

The advantages are that you do not have to pay service charges or ground rent. However, you will have to pay for all repairs and maintenance to the property.

New or old?

Despite the incentives offered by builders, older homes are increasingly popular with first-time buyers. A recent survey found that only a quarter of first-time buyers prefer a brand new home to a period property (built before 1945). Older homes are preferred because of their character, the fact that they are less uniform and are perceived to be better built. Even though new houses are efficiently heated, insulated, have modern plumbing and are easier to maintain and clean, the average homebuyer prefers to have sash windows (even if they are slighty draughty) and period features (even if that means poor plumbing and extra maintenance).

Part of the attraction is that older homes tend to be cheaper than new homes. And not only are older homes cheaper, but they tend to be more spacious.

New built

Buying from a builder can have its advantages:

- The price often includes extras such as a brand new fitted kitchen, curtains and carpets, and often builders will offer a special deal on a starter pack of furniture. At a time when you are strapped for cash this is a major advantage.

- Everything is brand new – you will not have to worry about an ancient boiler breaking down or replacing the kitchen or bathroom in a few years' time.

- You will not have to redecorate – and may even have a choice of colours of wallpaper and carpets and the type/colour of fixtures and fittings.

- You will not be involved in a chain – the vendor (in this case the builder) does not have to find another property to move into.

- There is less chance that you will be gazumped. Once you have seen a property and paid the deposit, you generally know that the property will be yours.

- The move will be easier to plan as you usually know exactly when you will be able to move in.

■ New homes are usually guaranteed by the National House Building Council (NHBC) against structural defects in the first 10 years. And for the first two years after the property has been built all defects in building work have to be put right by the builder at no cost to the buyer.

■ You don't need to pay for the more expensive full structural survey.

■ Running costs should be lower because newer homes are better insulated and do not need so much maintenance.

■ You may also be offered a larger mortgage than you would be able to get from a bank or building society as some builders offer 100 per cent home loans. However, watch out for the mortgage rate – it could be higher as a result.

However, there can be drawbacks:

■ Because new-built homes include extras such as a new kitchen and curtains and carpets, once you move in these then become second-hand. As such the property value can fall initially to reflect this. This can be a problem if you want to sell shortly after moving in and new homes are still being built in the area. After all, if you can buy brand new for the same price, there is no point in buying second-hand.

■ Newer homes tend to be built on new estates which often don't have the same facilities – such as a corner shop or local pub – as more established areas.

■ You may have to sacrifice some of the 'character' – older properties may boast high ceilings, period features and large windows.

■ Room sizes are often smaller than with older properties.

■ There may be delays in building schedules so you could find that you have to find temporary accommodation while waiting for building work to be completed.

> **Warning:** If you buy a new home make sure you report any defects in the quality of workmanship to the builders within the first two years, as after this only structural defects are covered by the NHBC warranty. So if doors or windows warp or don't fit properly, put your complaint in writing as soon as possible. Most new homes have minor problems so you must be prepared for these.

Buying off plan

The recent strength in the property market means that, increasingly, homebuyers have been purchasing properties before they are even built. Buyers view a show flat which gives an idea of what the property will look like and then pay a deposit on the particular house or flat that they want to buy. Buying usually involves:

■ viewing a show flat;

■ selecting a flat from a plan which shows its square footage and the size of rooms.

The advantages are:

■ If prices are rising you could make a profit before you even move in because the price you have agreed to pay is less than the market value a few months later when building work is completed.

■ You have plenty of time in which to plan your move.

■ You are often given a choice of colour schemes and can even have a say in how the kitchen is designed or where you want light fittings or electrical sockets to be placed.

The disadvantages are:

■ You will not have a true idea of how the property will look.

■ If building work is delayed you may have to find temporary accommodation until it is completed.

■ Show flats are carefully designed to make them appear larger and lighter. Often the beds, sofas and other furnishings are quite small to make rooms seem larger and once you move in your clutter, you may find the flat is much smaller than you first imagined. Some of the bedrooms may not be large enough to accommodate a double wardrobe – or even a double bed.

■ If the market is rising the developer may refund your deposit and sell the property for a higher price – so read the small print. Find out if – and under what circumstances – the developer can pull out.

Warning: Before parting with a deposit read the terms and conditions very carefully. If you have to pull out of the purchase you are unlikely to get your deposit refunded.

£ CASH TIP £

Several buyers have bought off plan and then sold the flat/house without ever moving in. If the property market is rising and prices increase in the time it takes to build the property, this is a way to make a few thousand pounds to finance your next purchase. However, there are pitfalls. You should be prepared to move into the property – once it is built prices could fall or you may not be able to find a buyer. And because most properties are now worth more on completion, some builders are reluctant to sell off plan. the other problem when prices are rising is that developers sometimes realize that they can sell the property for far more than originally agreed and may try to return your deposit so that they can make a bigger profit.

Older properties

Britain has the oldest stock of homes in Europe, with one in four properties built before the end of the First World War. Many of these have already been renovated, but there is still scope to buy an older home in need of improvement.

The advantages are:

■ Older properties tend to have higher ceilings, larger room sizes and bigger windows.

■ The property will be in an established area – so you will know what the area is like and will usually benefit from local shops, restaurants and bars.

■ The property will usually have more character.

■ You may be able to improve the property to enhance its value.

The disadvantages are:

■ The seller may be involved in a chain – trying to find, exchange and complete on another property – and in turn that vendor will have to do the same. This can make moving fraught and as such it may take you several attempts (with all the costs involved) to find a home that you can move into.

■ The running and maintenance costs are usually higher.

■ You will have to pay for a full or more detailed survey. When the new Home Information Packs (commonly known as seller's packs) are introduced in 2006, they will include a property condition report, which should highlight any major structural problems. Even so, if you are buying an older house you may want to commission and pay for your own survey to look into these problems in greater detail and to provide costs for any building works.

■ You will have to put up with the taste of the previous owner (even if this is only until you have time to redecorate).

■ You run the risk of expensive bills in future to replace things like the boiler or cooker or to repair rotten sash windows or a leaking roof.

Conversions

These are often a mixture of the old and the new. Large older homes are often divided into several flats, and during the conversion extensive modernization may mean that the flat appears like new.

The advantages are:

■ You get the period features of an older property, but with a modern or new bathroom and kitchen.

■ In more established areas where prices are high, you will probably not be able to stretch to buying a whole house. A conversion may enable you to afford the area of your choice.

The disadvantage is:

■ Much depends on the quality of the conversion. These large homes were not designed for multiple occupancy. As such you may be able to hear your neighbours walking around upstairs or you may find that your plasterboard walls offer little privacy.

Former offices/industrial buildings

Converting office blocks and old warehouses that are no longer needed for commercial purposes into residential apartments is increasingly popular in and around inner cities. Already, many wharf and water-side buildings have been converted into flats in London, Manchester and Liverpool.

The advantages of these are that:

■ they are usually centrally located, cutting down on commuting time;

- they often offer more space than comparable flats;

- concrete floors and solid walls usually mean they are quieter than conversions of residential properties;

- these homes are usually highly desirable so you should find them easy to resell;

- you can often buy properties in 'shell' form – you can then design the interior to suit your tastes and needs.

The disadvantages are:

- because these properties are desirable they are often very expensive;

- you often have to pay out substantial sums after moving in to pay for curtains, carpets and decoration; with 'shell' properties you will also have to pay for plumbing, wiring, kitchens and bathrooms and the building of internal walls.

Lofts

These New York-style open plan industrial flats started to become fashionable in London at the end of the 1980s and are now popular in most urban areas.

True lofts are converted old industrial buildings. However, loft-style apartments are now being built from scratch and offices, schools and even churches are being converted.

Generally, it is the quality of the building conversion – rather than the individual lofts – that affects the price. The exterior, windows, security and maintenance of the building will affect its long-term value more than decoration.

If you are buying a 'shell' apartment – which means you must build the interior including walls, and install plumbing, kitchens, wiring and bathrooms from scratch – you will need to ensure you have enough finance to cover these costs. A lender is only likely to lend on the basis that you can afford to turn the shell into a home. Basic fitting costs around £60 a square foot, although the sky is the limit. Building something unusual can either attract buyers or put them off and there is less of a chance that you will appeal to the maximum number of buyers.

Former council flats/houses

Tenants who bought through the Right to Buy scheme introduced by the Conservative Government in 1979 are now beginning to sell these council homes.

Although these tend to be far cheaper than other similar properties in an area, which may make them attractive for those who cannot afford anything else, there are some drawbacks.

The main problem is finance as many lenders are reluctant to advance mortgages on former council flats, because they can be hard to sell.

Another drawback can be the fact that the local council is the freeholder and therefore is responsible for repairs, service charges and maintenance of the estate/block. As such, the council is unlikely to pay for anything other than essential repairs – 24-hour porterage, a well stocked private garden and interior designed communal areas are something you are going to have to live without.

Before buying check:

■ How many flats/houses are already privately owned. Buying in a block or on an estate where there are a high number of owner occupiers will help when it comes to selling the property.

■ What plans the council has for the building. Remember, as with other leasehold properties you will have to pay service charges. So if extensive work is planned, you could face a huge increase in service charges. If there are only a few owner occupiers the service charges can be very high.

■ If the block/house is in a good area or surrounded by rundown, high-rise, poor quality housing. Pick the block and area carefully. As with all property purchases, location is the key.

Remember:

■ Low-rise flats are easier to sell than high-rise.

■ Ex-council homes can be difficult to resell.

■ Security is important. A flat in a block that has a bad reputation for crime and vandalism will be very difficult to resell.

■ Maintenance is another key factor. If you buy in a block where the lift is constantly breaking down or the grounds are strewn with rubbish and old furniture you will find it very difficult to sell your property.

Buying a run-down property

With a large number of homes in the UK falling below the government's tolerable standards, there is still plenty of scope to make money out of renovating an older property.

Remember, the costs of renovating a property quickly mount up to more than you budgeted for, take longer and are far more stressful. Often you will be better off paying more and having to do less work. What may be a profitable conversion for a builder could turn out to be unprofitable for the ordinary homebuyer.

There is often a very good reason why properties are cheap. Many run-down properties have been repossessed by mortgage lenders and may have either been left empty for several months or not benefited from maintenance and repairs because the cash-strapped homeowner could not afford these. In other cases, those faced with repossession strip their homes of everything from the bath to the kitchen to sell and raise much-needed cash.

Repossessions have been less plentiful in the past few years, and the number fell to just 4,270 in the first half of 2003 – a 20-year low.

They are sold either through estate agents, if they are in reasonable condition, or through residential property auctioneers.

If you are buying a property 'in need of modernization' or 'with room for improvement' always pay for a full structural survey and ask the surveyor to investigate specific areas of concern such as the roof or foundations.

Investigate how easy it will be to get planning consent. Then get accurate estimates for how much work will cost (and add another 10 per cent for contingencies). If the costs outweigh the additional value that will be added to the property, think again.

Warning: If a property is in need of even minor works – such as new guttering – the mortgage lender may withhold part of the mortgage advance until this work is completed, and give you either three or six months in which to prove that the work has been done to a satisfactory standard. If money is retained in this way you will not only have to find extra cash to meet the mortgage shortfall but will also have to pay for the repairs.

Finding a property

The term 'house-hunting' has never been more apt even in today's market. With as many as a dozen buyers after each property for sale, you will have to learn to hunt for a suitable property. And with gazumping (where another buyer snatches a property from you at the last minute by offering a higher price) you will also have to learn the hunter's instincts – be cunning, outwit your prey and be patient.

Approaching estate agents

Once you have decided what type of property you want, what you can afford and where you want to buy, approach as many estate agents as you can in the areas concerned. You may find that only a few specialize in the type or price of property that you are interested in.

With more potential buyers than there are sellers in many parts of the country, agents are reluctant to waste time on those who are 'just looking' and will favour those who are genuine buyers, so stress the following:

■ you are serious about buying;

■ you are a first-time buyer and as such are not in a chain (you will not have to find a buyer for your existing home);

■ you have mortgage finance in place so can move quickly (ask your lender to agree a mortgage for a certain amount 'in principle');

■ you are keen to move quickly and can view properties at short notice.

Try to establish a good rapport with the estate agent – that way he or she will think of you first when a property comes onto the market. Then tell the estate agent:

■ How much you can afford, and don't say you can offer more if you can't.

■ What you are looking for – you don't want to waste your own or the estate agent's time by viewing unsuitable properties. But don't be too specific. Remember you are unlikely to find a property that meets all your criteria within your price bracket.

■ How to get in touch with you at short notice (your work/home and mobile phone numbers). If you have access to a fax, ask if property details can be faxed to you rather than posted, to ensure you are one of the first to see a property.

Then keep in contact with the estate agent on a regular basis:

■ Ask the estate agent to inform you of any sales that have fallen through. The seller may be fed up and, if you are prepared to act quickly, you could find that you can move in a couple of weeks.

■ Keep pestering the estate agent to find out if there are any new properties coming on to his or her books. In areas where the number of buyers far outstrips the number of sellers, there is no point in asking the estate agent to ring you back. They are far too busy. It is up to you to ring them.

■ Don't waste the estate agent's time by asking to see properties you are not interested in. The agent may think you are not serious about buying and may be reluctant to show you properties in future, particularly if there are serious buyers prepared to put in sensible offers.

■ If a property comes onto the market, push to see the property that day – otherwise you may find that it is 'under offer' before you find time to view it.

The Internet: most estate agents now have Web sites so you can view property details online. Good picture quality and even panoramic video footage of rooms give you a good idea of what you are going to view. The only problem with Web sites is that some agents delay putting homes on their sites, so you are often better off using the old-fashioned telephone.

Property particulars

Once you have registered on their books, estate agents will then send you property details. It is essential that you respond to these as soon as possible. In the current market you may find that the property is already under offer (a price has been agreed) before you receive the particulars. That is why it is essential to telephone estate agents on a regular basis.

Under the Property Misdescriptions Act, what estate agents can say on property particulars is strictly regulated. The Act prevents estate agents from lying or giving false information about a property.

There will usually be a brief *description* of the type of property (flat or house), its age and location as well as whether it is leasehold or freehold. Other information that may be included is:

council tax, length of lease, service charges/ground rent and whether it is in good repair or in need of renovation.

Measurements should be accurate (they cannot add a couple of feet onto the size of a room) and are usually expressed as follows: 'living room 20ft × 16ft'. If the measurement says 'maximum' this means that the room is that large at its widest or longest point. So if it is L-shaped or has an alcove or bay window the room may be much smaller than the maximum measurements indicate.

The details will also include the *price*. If it is listed as 'ono' – this means 'or near offer' – you may have scope to offer less than the asking price.

The Act also requires estate agents to inform you if they have a personal interest in a property.

But while the Act requires estate agents to be honest, it does not require them to inform you of every defect with the property. You won't see property details saying 'desirable two-bedroom flat, slight damp problem, roof leaks when it rains and the boiler is on its last legs'. Remember, the estate agent is employed to present the property in the best light. And while agents must be truthful about things like distances and journey times, they are likely to verge on the side of optimism. So if a property is 10 minutes' walk from the station, you may find it takes you 15 or 20 minutes. And a 30-minute train journey from the nearest town or city may be 30 minutes only on a fast train.

However, if you ask (preferably in writing) a specific question about a property, the estate agent must give you an honest answer. Vendors, on the other hand, can lie – so don't take their word for anything. Remember, the golden rule is *caveat emptor*, or buyer beware.

The Act does not prevent estate agents from using their own terminology to describe a home. Property particulars nearly always begin with 'spectacular', 'spacious', 'charming', 'stunning' or another flattering word or phrase.

Although estate agents have toned down the more misleading euphemisms, they still use terms like:

'Scope for improvement' – a lot of work will be needed so you will either need a lot of money or be a DIY enthusiast.

'Much sought after' – either it will probably be sold before you get to view it or the estate agent wants you to think that it will.

'Requires modernization' – does not have central heating and maybe even still have an outside loo.

'Cottage' – small.

'Bijou' – even smaller.

'Near station' – trains run at the back of your garden.

'Convenient for local bars and restaurants' – it's next door to a noisy pub.

'Light and airy' – lots of large draughty windows.

The key to reading property particulars is to look at what they don't say. If service charges are not mentioned, does that mean they are so high they may be offputting? And read between the lines. If you are sent details about a fifth-floor flat, why isn't the lift mentioned? Perhaps there isn't one. Remember that while a photograph may be enclosed, it may be taken from a very flattering angle or cropped (the tower block on the left may no longer be visible).

Problems with estate agents

A few estate agents have been accused of accepting payments from buyers desperate to secure a deal on a property and avoid being gazumped. Under the National Association of Estate Agents' code, estate agents are not allowed to accept payments from buyers as well as sellers. However, if the agent is acting only for a buyer a homefinder's fee can be paid.

The other reported scam is for agents to inform buyers that there have been higher offers made on the property. These turn out to be fictitious, but as agents work on a commission basis they have every incentive to push the price higher.

If you have exhausted your estate agent's complaints procedure and are still not happy, contact the Ombudsman for Estate Agents on 01722 333306. They can award compensation of up to £25,000 if they rule in favour of the complainant. But note: not every estate agent is a member of the Ombudsman Scheme, so check first.

Other ways to find a property

Although using an estate agent is likely to be the best option – after all you don't have to pay the commission and as such the service costs you nothing – there are other ways to find a property.

Advertisements in papers

Your local paper will be the ideal place to find out about new property developments. Most papers run a weekly property section or page with a mixture of editorial and advertisements.

Builders often advertise their new developments in papers rather than selling through estate agents. The adverts will tell you about open days (days when you can view the properties) and any special incentives offered (such as 100 per cent home loans or free kitchen appliances).

Private sales – where the vendor does not want the expense of employing an estate agent – are also usually advertised in newspapers.

Using an agent

If you are finding it hard to buy a property you can employ an agent to act on your behalf, paying a fee of between 1.5 and 2 per cent of the purchase price. Although this adds to the cost of buying, agents can often find properties that are not on the open market and the attraction of this arrangement is that the vendor does not have to pay estate agency fees (unless they have already signed up with an estate agent, in which case the agent may insist on still charging the fee).

Buying at auction

As a first-time buyer you may not want to take the risk of buying at auction. Inexperienced househunters usually lose out to the professional property developers who know how to get the best deal. If you do succeed in buying a property it may be because those in the know wouldn't touch such a bad investment.

Pros:

▪ If you are successful you could buy a property for far less than through an estate agent.

▪ You can often buy a more unusual property – such as a former railway station or an old police house.

Cons:

▪ There is often a reason why properties are sold at auction rather than through an estate agent – properties tend to be in much poorer repair, in less desirable areas, may have subsidence or are uninsurable, may be in a noisy area or have a restrictive lease. Squatters may have left the property in a poor state or it may be a repossession that has been left empty for several months. If this is the case then you may find it hard to get a mortgage.

▪ You should pay for a survey, legal searches and a valuation before making your bid, but could find this money is wasted because you have been outbid.

▪ If the property needs extensive work you should also find out about any planning requirements you will need to meet.

How to buy at auction: The first rule is don't. If you have found a property you want to buy, ask the vendors if they are willing to sell prior to the auction. If this isn't an option, apply the following rules:

▪ Sign up with as many auctioneers as possible.

▪ If you see a property that appeals in a catalogue, ask the auctioneer for all the information about that property.

▪ Find out the guide price from the auctioneer – this will be close to the reserve price and will give you an indication of how much you are likely to have to pay.

▪ Look over the property yourself.

∎ Keep in touch with the auctioneer to check that the property is still for sale. You don't want to pay out for survey and legal fees, only to find that the property has been withdrawn from the auction.

∎ Arrange your finance. You can usually apply for a mortgage and receive an agreement in principle. The lender will require a valuation by an approved valuer, a survey (a full survey in most cases) and legal and planning searches in advance. Remember, you will have to pay these fees even if the sale falls through. You may find that the property is in such poor repair that it is unmortgageable. Also, remember to budget for the 10 per cent deposit, legal and professional fees, stamp duty and the cost of repairs.

∎ You should instruct a solicitor to handle the conveyancing and searches as you will have to give the solicitor's name and address to the auctioneer if your bid is accepted.

∎ Contact an insurer to find out if there will be any problems insuring the property.

At the auction:

∎ Get there early to find out if there are any last minute changes.

∎ Set yourself a maximum bidding limit – so you don't get carried away and bid more than you can afford.

∎ If your bid is accepted, you will usually be required to pay a 10 per cent deposit immediately the bid is accepted. You will then have 28 days to pay the final balance. Find out what form of payment the auctioneer accepts.

∎ Remember, if your bid is accepted you have entered into a binding contract.

∎ Leasehold properties require a detailed study of the lease with solicitors' advice.

∎ If the property is a repossession you must also check that you are not liable for any unpaid ground rents or service charges.

For further information: The Incorporated Society of Valuers and Auctioneers, 3 Cadogan Gate, London, SW1X 0AS (telephone 020 7235 2282) produces a leaflet giving guidelines for anyone buying or selling their home at auction.

Viewing a property

Once you have been sent property particulars by estate agents (or seen a property advertised in a newspaper), you then move on to the next stage in the house-hunting process.

As a first-time buyer it is essential that you don't buy the first property you see unless it really is your ideal home. You should view a few properties just so that you get to know what is on offer.

You must make an appointment to view with the estate agent. If you are one of the first to view you will have a better chance of making the first offer that is accepted.

The estate agent will often come with you to view the property (particularly on the first viewing) or may arrange for you to view when the vendors are at home.

Remember, you can view a property more than once. If you are interested in the property – or have already made an offer – you can view again to check that your first impressions were right or to measure up to see if your furniture will fit.

If you cannot make an appointment make sure you cancel in plenty of time. If you don't, you will annoy the estate agent and the vendor.

When to view

If you can, drive past the property and view it from the outside on different days of the week and at different times. That way you can find out what the early morning or late evening traffic is like and if it is a 'rat run', how easy it is to park the car at night, if there are any noisy neighbours and if the trains/buses/tubes that run nearby make so much noise you could not sleep at night.

Viewing at different times will also let you see how light affects the property. You may find that even on a sunny morning the property looks dark and dingy or that the garden never gets any sun because of overlooking properties. Things to look out for include:

■ Nearby pubs, cinemas, sports grounds, restaurants or other entertainment facilities that could cause problems with noise, rubbish, congestion and parking.

■ Nearby houses that are unkempt or derelict – they could affect local property values or, worse, become squats.

■ Nearby properties with cracks in the brickwork – this could be an indication that the area suffers from subsidence.

■ Street lighting – is the area well lit and safe to walk around at night?

■ Are there any large trees near the property? These could cause subsidence.

■ Is the property exposed or secluded?

■ Are there any geographical features that could affect the property – if it is on a steep hill will you want to walk up it every night after a hard day's work; are there any streams or rivers that could cause flooding?

What to take

When viewing a property, take with you the estate agent's particulars, a notepad and pen and a tape measure. The tape measure is so you can check your sofa/bed/wardrobe/bookshelves will fit into a particular space. It will also be useful to check the estate agent's details – these are often given as maximum dimensions or as an overall square footage.

Also make up a list of questions you want to ask or points you want to check. For instance:

▌ Will the carpets and curtains be included in the sale?

▌ What type of central heating system is installed and how old is it?

▌ What items of kitchen equipment will be sold with the property – it is usual for fitted cookers to be included, but not always fridges, dishwashers or washing machines.

A more detailed list is included in the section on 'Conveyancing – what questions to ask'.

Viewing from outside

Most people make up their mind whether or not they will buy a property in a matter of minutes. Viewing the property from outside will give you a good indication of whether or not this is the type of property you will be interested in buying.

You should also take a few minutes to look at the following:

▌ the state of the roof;

▌ whether or not there are any obvious cracks in the walls (indications of subsidence);

▌ the state of repair of the windows;

▌ the quality of security (if it is a block of flats, is the communal front door kept locked?);

▌ parking facilities or availability of street parking;

▌ state of repair of party walls/fences or communal gardens/walkways.

Viewing inside the property

First impressions can often be misleading. Don't be put off by the existing owner's decor – you can always change that. Or you may feel that this is the perfect property only to find that when you move in there is not enough storage space.

If you are looking inside a new home or show flat, the furniture may be arranged to give the illusion that the property is larger than it is. When you move in a king-size bed you may find there is no room in the bedroom for anything else.

The following are often overlooked:

■ Light – is there enough natural light and where does the sun shine into the flat/house and at what time of day?

■ Storage – is there somewhere to store your suitcases/bicycle/filing cabinet?

■ Wardrobes – are these fitted or will you have to buy your own and, if so, is there enough room?

■ Noise – can you hear the neighbours/cars driving past the property? If the walls are made of plasterboard you may find that you have little privacy within the property.

■ Central heating – what type is it, how long has it been installed and are there sufficient radiators? Remember that what seems a light and airy home in summer can be a dark and cold place in the winter.

■ Electrical fittings – are there enough electrical sockets and are they conveniently placed?

■ Kitchen – is it practical? Could you actually cook a meal in it, is there adequate ventilation, is there enough space to fit a washing machine and a tumble dryer and if you are planning to live with someone else can you both fit in the kitchen at the same time?

■ Dining – is there somewhere to eat? Is there enough room to entertain?

■ Plumbing – turn on a couple of taps (or ask to use the bathroom) to find out if the plumbing is noisy and if the hot water works.

■ Laundry – is there a washing machine, will it be left by the present owners, is there somewhere to dry/air clothes?

■ Bathroom – is there a shower or room to fit a power shower? Is there enough room to store towels and toiletries?

■ Neighbours – it is very difficult to find out if there are problem neighbours before buying a property. But it is worth doing a bit of detective work as you could end up living in misery because of loud music, a noisy dog or damp because your neighbour has failed to maintain his or her property. Yet only 16 per cent of buyers are worried about their future neighbours, even though they can make life hell and affect the future saleability of the property.

Other things to consider

Repair costs: Look for items that might be expensive to repair: windows, floors, roof, electrics, damp, central heating and cracks in the walls.

Running costs: Few homebuyers check the running costs of the property, but these can often mean the difference between easily affording to buy and struggling. Costs to consider include:

■ heating – large draughty rooms and rotting or ill-fitting windows can make heating bills soar and leave you in a cold unwelcoming home in winter;

■ council tax;

■ insurance – some postcode areas are very expensive because of high crime rates or increased risks of subsidence;

■ service charges and ground rent if you are buying a leasehold property.

Living costs: If you move far away from work your travelling costs can easily mount up and if there are no local supermarkets you may find that buying your food at the local corner shop works out to be very expensive.

9 Once you have found a property: offers, searches, valuations and surveys

Making an offer

If, after viewing a property, you decide you want to buy it, make your decision quickly. If you dither you may find that someone else has already made an offer that has been accepted or you could be gazumped.

Before making an offer remember this: *Buy with your brain not your heart.* Ask yourself:

■ Do I really want to live there?

■ Could I cope with commuting from that distance?

■ Can I really afford to live there? Remember running costs as well as purchase costs.

■ Does the property meet most of my requirements?

If you want to make an offer tell the estate agent and ask to be informed as soon as possible if your offer has been accepted. You must inform the estate agent, not the vendor, so that the agent can tell other potential buyers that the property is under offer and stop showing other potential buyers round the property.

In the current property market most buyers offer less than the asking price by as much as 10 per cent. Be prepared for the vendor to refuse the offer, so that you may have to come back with a higher offer.

When you make an offer and it is accepted, this is not a binding contract (other than in Scotland). Either you – or the vendor – can pull out of the agreement at any time until exchange of contracts. This is when you pay a deposit on the property and the sale is confirmed.

So when you make an offer make sure it is 'subject to contract'. This means you can pull out if:

■ The survey shows that the property is in a poor condition (for instance it is suffering from damp or subsidence) or needs extensive work. In this case you can either withdraw your offer or make a lower offer.

■ You are unable to raise the required mortgage.

■ The local authority searches show that the property value and your enjoyment of the property may be affected in some way – for instance a major road will be built through your back garden.

■ You simply change your mind.

Making an offer 'subject to contract' gives you no protection against being gazumped or the vendor pulling out of the sale – which could cost you up to £1,000 in wasted legal and surveying fees. But it does have its compensations. This system protects you from being committed to buying a property that later turns out to be suffering from major problems. So if the vendor objects to agreeing to a purchase on a 'subject to contract' basis be wary. Do not sign any contract at this stage of the buying process without taking legal advice.

If your offer is accepted set an early date for exchange of contracts, to avoid the risk of being gazumped.

Warning: Despite a slow-down in property price growth, buyers still find themselves under pressure to make a quick decision. Do not be pushed into making a panic purchase. Remember, there is nothing to stop you making an offer and then withdrawing it should you change your mind. If you are buying in an area where there is a shortage of affordable first-time buyer homes then make your offer quickly – other buyers may get in there first. Try to view properties as soon as they come onto the market and put in any offer before the weekend, when most viewers tend to look around the property. There is nothing to stop you putting in a lower offer and then, if this is rejected, upping it at a later date. You cannot lower your offer price as easily.

Once your offer has been accepted

If your offer is accepted it is important to put pressure on your solicitor, surveyor and estate agent to push the sale through as quickly as possible to avoid the risk of gazumping. Then:

1   Inform your mortgage lender so that:
    ▮ the final amount of loan can be agreed
    ▮ the lender can tell you how to arrange a valuation of the property (this can often be combined with a survey); you may have to use a valuer from a panel approved by the lender
    ▮ a provisional date for the mortgage to be advanced can be agreed.
2   Instruct your solicitor to proceed with conveyancing to exchange of contracts:
    ▮ give details of the property address
    ▮ give the name of the vendor's solicitor (ask the estate agent)
    ▮ give details of your mortgage lender

▌ tell the solicitor roughly how quickly you wish to proceed and when you expect to move into the property.

3 Arrange for a surveyor/valuer to inspect the property (when the seller's packs are introduced in 2006 you may not need to do this – however, a full structural survey will still be recommended for older houses).

4 Give notice (if you have not done so already) that you will be moving out of your current accommodation.

5 In some cases you may be required to pay a preliminary deposit (particularly if you are buying from a builder). If the estate agent asks for a deposit (say £250 as a token of your intent) remember that this deposit has no legal standing and does not bind you to the transaction. Make sure you get a receipt and if you sign anything make sure it says the deposit is paid 'subject to contract and to survey'.

£ CASH TIP £

Make sure you have legal expenses insurance included in your household insurance policy (see the section on insuring your home in chapter 12). However, this will not cover disputes that started before the policy was taken out (such as problems with your survey).

How long will it take from making an offer to moving in?

The average time between a property being on the market to an offer being accepted and the buyer moving in can vary from one week to one year – depending on the type of property and its location and whether or not it is priced competitively. Some properties are snapped up quickly while others languish on the market for months.

Once an offer has been accepted, it generally takes around 12 weeks for contracts to be exchanged. However, as a first-time buyer you will not be in a 'chain' (you will have no property to sell), so this can be completed in just four weeks. However, you will have to put pressure on your solicitor. The buyers may not want to proceed so quickly if they need to find another property. Once contracts have been exchanged you will then have an average of just three weeks to arrange the move before completion.

Tip: If you have found your dream home you can offer to wait for it. To secure the property push to exchange contracts as quickly as possible (a 10 per cent deposit is usually paid but this may be reduced by negotiation) and agree to an extended completion – for example, three months. This secures the property and gives the vendors a guaranteed sale putting them in a stronger position when negotiating to buy their next home.

Conveyancing: legal searches and checks

What is conveyancing?

Conveyancing is the legal process by which the right of ownership of the property (the title of the property) is transferred. There are two stages:

▌ from acceptance of your offer up to exchange of contracts;

▌ from exchange of contracts to completion.

Once contracts have been exchanged neither the buyer nor seller can pull out. The process can take anything from 48 hours to two months or more.

The first stage involves vital checks, including what is included in the purchase price, whether any planning applications will affect the property and if there are any restrictions on the use of the property. Your solicitor/conveyancer should check the following:

■ *The vendor has the right to sell the property* – this will usually be done by checking the Land Registry.

■ *The property is not subject to any outstanding undisclosed 'charges'* – this means that no other person or institution has a right to the proceeds of the sale of the property and no loans (other than any mortgage that will be repaid with the proceeds of the sale) are charged against the property.

■ *The property is sold with vacant possession* – when the seller leaves it will be empty and ready for you to occupy and there are no 'sitting' tenants.

Your solicitor will also ask the vendor's solicitor to complete a questionnaire which will include the following points:

What is included in the sale: Generally, anything that is part of the fabric of the property is included in the sale, but there can be disputes. It is not unknown for some vendors to remove inbuilt dishwashers, curtain rails, light fittings, fitted cupboards and even fireplaces. The usual rule is that if it is not removable without causing damage it is part of the structure of the property and it is included in the sale. But it is safer to check.

Your solicitor will ask specific questions about many items – these are listed on a standard form which the vendor must complete. However, it may still be advisable to go through the property with the vendor agreeing what is included in the sale shortly after you have made your offer. Put the list in writing and give a copy to your solicitor. If not, make sure that the list of items included and excluded in the sale sent out by your solicitor includes any items that you are specifically interested in ensuring are part of the sale. And don't be fobbed off by replies which say 'see estate agent's particulars' or are vague.

There can be areas of dispute. Check the following:

■ Kitchen – if there are any free-standing items such as a slot-in cooker, fridge, dishwasher or washing machine, remember these are not always included in the sale.

▌ Wardrobes – usually if they are fitted, they are included in the sale – but not always. If they are part of a matching set of furniture the vendor may want to take them.

▌ Garden – some sellers even go as far as digging up plants. If the greenhouse or garden shed is built on foundations it should be included in the sale.

▌ Carpets – these are usually included in the sale (occasionally vendors ask for an extra amount to pay for these) but rugs are not.

▌ Light fittings – check whether the vendor plans to remove lamp shades (most do) and any light fittings including wall lamps (most don't). Be prepared for some vendors to go as far as removing all the light bulbs.

▌ Curtains – these are often negotiated as a separate sale.

▌ Shelves – if these are to be removed make sure that the vendor 'makes good' any damage to the walls or plaster.

▌ Bathroom fittings – if the bathroom cabinets, towel rails and toilet roll holders are fitted they should generally be included in the sale. However, some vendors do take them with them.

▌ TV aerial – satellite dishes are often removed and occasionally even the TV aerial.

Don't forget to check that the agreed items have been left by the vendor and that the items are still the same and have not been exchanged for cheap, second-hand goods.

Make sure the list of what is included in the sale is agreed early on in the conveyancing procedure as it may affect the price you are prepared to pay for the property or you may have to raise extra cash to pay for curtains and carpets.

Your solicitor or conveyancer will need to know the details of any items in the house which you have agreed to buy as an extra.

It is also not uncommon for buyers to find that they have inherited certain items they do not want. The vendor may leave behind an old wardrobe, shelving units or a dirty old carpet. Make sure you agree that all items of furniture are removed, just in case the vendor has other ideas.

Whether there are any guarantees: Your solicitor or conveyancer should ask if there are any guarantees covering:

▪ the damp course;

▪ any treatment for woodrot/woodworm;

▪ any items of major work – such as a new roof;

▪ the boiler/central heating system;

▪ any wiring/plumbing/electrical items, etc.

Where the boundaries of the property lie: Boundary disputes can cause major problems and even lead to court cases between neighbours. Don't assume that fences, hedges and walls give a true indication of the boundary of the property.

Your solicitor should give you a plan showing exactly where the boundaries lie and who is responsible for maintaining any boundary walls or fences. Some property deeds can be vague, so make sure you measure carefully to check boundaries are in the correct place.

There may be obligations or conditions specified in the deeds, for instance a minimum or maximum height of any fence, whose responsibility it is to repair any fence or wall or whether or not boundary fences or hedges are allowed.

If there are any restrictive covenants: There may be a restriction on what the property can be used for, that it cannot be let, that no pets may be kept or that you are required to paint the property in a particular colour. Your solicitor/conveyancer should check that these are not unduly restrictive.

That there are no outstanding disputes regarding the property: There could be disputes regarding boundaries or planning applications. The solicitor should also check that any additions to the property – such as an extension – have met local planning requirements and that building regulation consent was obtained.

If there are any rights of way or rights of access: This involves checking that you don't have a public right of way or footpath through the grounds of the property and if you have shared rights of access with a neighbour – for instance to a driveway or garden.

Conveyancing changes

When the new Home Information Packs (HIPs, also known as seller's packs) are introduced in 2006, conveyancing will be much faster as much of the work will already have been completed by the vendor.

The HIPs will include information about:

- terms of sale;
- evidence of title;
- replies to standard searches;
- planning consents, agreements and directions and building control certificates;
- replies to preliminary enquiries made on behalf of buyers;
- a home condition report based on a professional survey of the property including an energy efficiency assessment;
- for new properties – copies of warranties and guarantees;
- for leasehold properties – a copy of the lease, most recent service charge accounts and receipts, building insurance policy details and payment receipts, regulations made by the landlord or management company and the memorandum and articles of the landlord or management company.

This information is already obtained under the current conveyancing process. However, the vendor will now do it before the property is put up for sale – speeding up the entire process and reducing the cost for the buyer.

Although the new HIPs will not become compulsory until 2006 (dependent on the legislation being passed in time), they are likely to be adopted on a voluntary basis before then, so you could find that a pack has already been produced by the vendor.

Local authority searches

One of the solicitor's or conveyancer's jobs is to request local searches to check that there are no plans in the pipeline that may affect the value or future enjoyment of the home you are buying. If a major road is about to be built near your new home or a large superstore is being built on land nearby you will want to know about it so you can either pull out of the purchase or negotiate a lower price.

Local searches are charged on a flat fee basis and usually cost around £170. However, if you live in an area that may need an extra geological search – for instance if there has been extensive mining in the past – this will cost extra.

There used to be long delays in waiting for local searches to be completed by local authorities, with some taking weeks or even months. The average time today is only a few weeks. If you need to exchange contracts before the search has been completed it is possible to take out an insurance policy to cover you against any negative information the search may have uncovered. Your solicitor/conveyancer should be able to give you details.

In some cases the vendor may request a local authority search at the time of putting the property on the market. This speeds up the process and the costs are eventually borne by the buyer.

Warning: There can be flaws in this process. Local authority searches only cover the property itself and will now show up information about nearby property that may be demolished to make way for a tower block. You may fall in love with a home because of its view but the search may not uncover that this may soon be spoilt by a new development, because the land is not near enough to show up on the search.

Remember, when the Channel Tunnel rail link was proposed thousands of homes in London and the South East were blighted, but the proposals did not appear on local authority searches.

> **Tip:** If there is any unused land or there are any derelict properties nearby, you can ask the owners and local residents if they know of any plans for development.

Land Registry searches

The title of the property is usually checked through the Land Registry, the official register of land ownership. Nine in ten properties are listed on its database. If it is registered the owner will have a Land Certificate (or Charge Certificate if the property is mortgaged). This certificate gives all the information held at the Land Registry including:

- a site plan (showing the size and location of the property);
- the ownership or proprietorship register;
- a charges register showing if there are any outstanding rights over the property (for instance a mortgage or loan secured against it).

If the property is not registered, ownership is proved by the production of the title deeds.

The solicitor or conveyancer will also register the transfer of ownership of the property into your name with the Land Registry. The fees for this are paid by the buyer and range from £40 to £500, depending on the value of the property.

Buying a new property

If you are buying a newly built home your solicitor/conveyancer should also check:

■ that the boundaries of the property are as shown on the plan;

■ that the size of the property is as shown;

■ that services are provided/connected;

■ that the contract provides for the house to be properly built to the specification;

■ whether there are any rights of way over the property;

■ that the local authority has agreed to the construction of roads and, once they are built, will take them over (if the road is not maintained by the council, residents will have to foot the bill);

■ whether there are any restrictions – such as the fact that no fences or garden boundaries can be built;

■ that planning permission was obtained, complied with and did not contain any restrictive conditions;

■ that drainage and sewerage will be taken over and maintained by the relevant utility.

Leasehold properties

If you are buying a leasehold property the conveyancing will also involve the transfer of the lease from the vendor to the purchaser. As such your solicitor should check:

■ that the lease does not have any restrictions that may affect the value or your future enjoyment of the property;

■ that the current leaseholder is up-to-date on service charge and ground rent payments;

■ that there are no problems with the lease that could affect the future saleability of the property.

Valuations

Your lender will require a valuation of the property usually by a firm on its approved panel of surveyors. This is to ensure that the property is adequate security for the loan and that the mortgage advance is not greater than the value of the property or greater than a certain percentage of its value (for instance if you are taking out a 95 per cent mortgage).

Warning: The overheating of the property market in some areas means that even if you think the property you are buying is 'worth' the amount you are paying, your lender may not. Valuers were caught out in the 1988 house price boom when they overvalued some properties and, as a result, they are now more conservative. However, it is still unlikely that the lender's valuation will be lower than the price you have offered. If it is you will either have to find the extra cash to meet the shortfall (lenders will only advance mortgages on the amount set by the valuer) or worse, you may have to pull out of the purchase.

Surveys

In more than 80 per cent of purchases, homebuyers rely on the valuation and buy without a thorough survey. They may pay tens or even hundreds of thousands of pounds for a home, but are not prepared to ensure that this investment is sound by spending a few hundred pounds on a full survey.

Unless you are buying a newly built or recently built house, or a flat in a modern block, you should consider paying for a survey. If there is a major fault with the building this survey can save you thousands of pounds in the long run. Even if there are only minor faults, a survey can still pay as you may be able to negotiate a reduction in the asking price.

If you fail to have a survey not only will you have little idea of the amount of work that may be required, but may have no means of redress should you find that there are major problems.

Surveys by vendors

In future a survey will be paid for by the vendor – before the property is put onto the market – and this will be included in the new Home Information Packs (HIPs), which will become compulsory from 2006.

The home condition report based on a professional survey of the property should provide buyers of most homes with adequate information – and more information than they currently receive in the valuation report. However, those purchasing older properties may want more detailed surveys. For example, if the report included in the HIP highlights a problem with damp or the roof, they may want to purchase a further report and ask for estimates of the cost of repairs.

'Caveat emptor' – or buyer beware

Agents – but not individuals – are obliged to be truthful when advertising and marketing properties under the Properties Misdescription Act 1991. This may give you some comfort, but if you are not relying on a survey but what the vendor tells you, you could be left seriously out of pocket. Even estate agents are not obliged to disclose more than they feel like disclosing.

So if the estate agent knows there has been a negative survey which led to a potential buyer pulling out, that agent does not have to tell you. However, if you ask you must be told the truth. If the estate agent lies, he or she is breaking the law. If you ask the vendors and they lie, you may be able to sue them – but it will cost you. Compensation will be based on what the property would have been worth had the problem been known – which is often only a few hundred or thousand pounds, not the true cost to you.

To pin a vendor down make sure your solicitor asks the usual questions and if the responses (which should be in writing) are vague, see if further questions can be asked. For example, if the vendors are asked if there have been any complaints made against neighbours for noise nuisance they could answer 'no' if they have only made verbal complaints and have not contacted the local authority's environmental health department. You could then move in and find yourself living next to the neighbours from hell.

To be safe never rely on what you are told – check for yourself. Ask for copies of warranties and guarantees. Do not rely on being told verbally that an appliance is under guarantee. Get the central heating inspected by a gas engineer rather than assuming that when the vendors say the heating works fine they are telling the truth. You could end up living in a house that is freezing in winter, because of inadequate heating.

Different types of survey

The valuation report

Sometimes paid for by the lender, it usually costs between £150 and £200. This is a valuation. Although you, as the buyer, must usually pay for it, it is designed to reassure the lender that the property is worth enough to cover the amount of the loan should you default on the mortgage payments.

The valuation report will only outline any serious problems that affect the value of the property. So if the home is suffering from subsidence or damp this should be pointed out.

In a few cases the valuer may value the property at less than the asking or agreed purchase price. As a result, the amount the lender is prepared to lend may be reduced.

If major or substantial repairs are required on the property, the lender will probably withhold a proportion of the mortgage until these works have been completed. Often a time limit – say three or six months – is given in which these repairs or renovations must be carried out.

> **Warning:** If the lender retains (holds back) some of the mortgage advance awaiting completion of necessary works, you could find that you cannot afford the property. Not only will you have to find the cash for the repairs, you will also have to make up (even if only on a temporary basis) for the shortfall in the mortgage.

The homebuyers' survey and valuation

As a rough guide, this costs around £400. It is more detailed than the valuation report and is often completed at the same time as the valuation and by the same surveyor. However, it is not what is commonly referred to as a 'full survey'. It is also known as the House Purchase and Valuation report, the Home Buyers' Survey and Valuation (HBSV or HSV) and a Scheme Two Survey.

The survey is completed on a standard form and is designed to pick up major faults. The survey will also tell you if there are any items of work that you will need to undertake shortly after moving in. Although the report should point out any damp, woodrot or woodworm, the surveyor will probably not inspect under floorboards or in the roof.

Note: An HSV is not a detailed survey of every aspect of the property and focuses only on major and urgent matters including details of:

■ the property's general condition;

■ any major faults, in accessible parts of the property, that may affect its value;

■ urgent and significant matters that need assessing before exchanging contracts (or before making an offer in Scotland) including recommendations for any further specialist inspections;

■ results of any testing of walls for dampness;

- comments on damage to timbers including woodworm or rot;

- comments on the existence and condition of damp-proofing, insulation and drainage (although drains are not tested);

- the recommended costs of reconstructing a building in the event of damage (such as fire) for insurance purposes. This is not the same as the market value of the property;

- the value of the property on the open market.

Building or full structural survey

This costs upwards of £400. It is recommended for those buying older properties, conversions of older properties, and unusual homes, as well as those planning to undertake any renovations. It can be combined with the valuation, although this is often done separately. You can usually save money by combining the two types of survey, provided the lender accepts the surveyor's valuation. If you have any particular concerns point these out to the surveyor and ask for a more detailed inspection. Put your request in writing, so if a fault appears after you have moved in you can claim redress from the surveyor.

A building survey includes details of:

- major and minor faults;

- the implications of any possible faults and the possible cost of repairs;

- results of any testing of walls for dampness;

- comments on damage to timbers including woodworm or rot;

- comments on the existence and condition of damp-proofing, insulation and drainage (although drains are not tested);

- extensive technical information on the construction of the property and details about material used;

- information on the location;

- recommendations for any further special inspections.

If you need help in finding a Chartered Surveyor, search the Royal Institute of Chartered Surveyors Web site at www.ricsfirms.co.uk or contact the call centre on 0870 333 1600. The RICS holds details of nearly 20,000 firms across the United Kingdom.

New homes

If you are buying a new property or a recently built home it will probably be covered by a 10-year warranty. These are issued when homes are first built, but are transferred to new owners if the house is sold within the warranty period.

There are two types of warranty: The National House Building Council (NHBC) and The Zurich Municipal warranty.

If you are buying a newer home you may feel that you can dispense with a survey. However, one may still be advisable if the warranty is nearing its end. The NHBC 'Buildmark' cover will pay for the cost of any work not properly completed by the builder within the first two years. After that it won't pay for anything that was or could have been reported to the builder.

A home condition report required as part of the Home Information Pack (to be introduced in 2006) may not be required, although at the time of writing this has yet to be finalized.

▌ you move in and find that the roof is leaking;

▌ when you pull up the old carpets you find the floorboards are rotten;

▌ when clearing out under the stairs you find that there is damp;

▌ fuses keep blowing and you employ an electrician who tells you the wiring is dangerous.

You may think that you have a good case against your surveyor, but if you read your survey report you may find otherwise. The surveyor may have written 'unable to inspect floorboards as property had fitted carpets' or 'roof not inspected as could not get access'. Unless you specifically asked the surveyor to check these points you may find you have no case.

Even if you do, you will then have to prove that the surveyor was negligent and that the defect should have been one that a skilled professional ought to have spotted.

The Royal Institute of Chartered Surveyors requires that all members have a complaints-handling procedure.

If you find that the member does not have a complaints procedure in place, you should contact the RICS Professional Conduct team who will ensure your complaint is dealt with correctly:

RICS Professional Conduct
PO Box 2291
Coventry CV4 8ZJ

020 7695 1580

If you have been through a firm's internal complaints-handling procedure you may still wish to bring your complaint to the attention of RICS so that it can investigate a particular aspect of a member's behaviour.

Please note that RICS can consider only those matters falling within its code of conduct, for example:

■ a delay in dealing with your affairs;

■ failure or a delay in replying to letters;

■ disclosure of confidential information;

■ failure to disclose a conflict of interest;

■ failure to look after your money;

■ failure to have a complaints procedure.

RICS cannot comment on or investigate cases where the law provides a remedy. It cannot therefore assess or award compensation. If your complaint concerns professional negligence or breach of contract you should take the matter up with the firm, ideally consulting a solicitor or the Citizens Advice Bureau. If you are seeking compensation of £5,000 or less you can consider taking your case to the small claims court.

An alternative to court action is arbitration. Arbitration is a process carried out by an independent person (an arbitrator) who will consider both sides of the case in a less formal way than in a court of law. His or her decision will be binding and can be enforced in a court of law. Further details are available from the Chartered Institute of Arbitrators on 020 7421 7444.

Complaints you may have against your lender

If your lender has left you out of pocket by changing the terms of the mortgage at the last minute, or by making an administrative error that caused delays and extra costs, you should initially complain to the complaints department at the head office. As a last resort, you can take your case to the:

Financial Ombudsman Service
South Quay Plaza
183 Marsh Wall
London E14 9SR
08450 80 1800

The service is free and you must complain to your bank or building society first.

Complaints you may have against your solicitor/conveyancer

If you have received a poor quality or slow service, or feel the service was negligent, you may be able to complain to:

The Office for the Supervision of Solicitors
Victoria Court
8 Dormer Place
Leamington Spa
Warwickshire
CV32 5AE
0845 608 6565
www.oss.lawsociety.org.uk

or

The Council for Licensed Conveyancers
16 Glebe Road
Chelmsford
Essex
CM1 1QG
01245 349599
www.conveyancer.org.uk

Under the Office for the Supervision of Solicitors scheme you can receive compensation or a refund of fees up to £1,000. If you want to complain about how the Law Society Office for the Supervision of Solicitors dealt with your complaint contact:

The Legal Services Ombudsman
3rd Floor
Sunlight House
Quay Street
Manchester
M33JZ

0845 601 0794
www.olso.org.uk

As a last resort you may want to make a claim against your solicitor's or conveyancer's negligence insurance. The Law Society has a panel of solicitors who will take on cases against other solicitors. Apply to:

The Law Society
113 Chancery Lane
London
WC2A 1PL

020 7242 1222

Complaints you may have against a house-builder

As discussed earlier in this book, even when moving into a new property you should expect problems. Few new homes are sold without some needing some minor repairs, even if these are only adjusting a door fitting or replacing a chipped tile.

Follow the claim procedure under your NHBC or other guarantee and make sure you put all complaints in writing.

Most likely problems

Heating failure is the most common home emergency, according to the Home Assistance arm of Internet and telephone insurer, esure.

Two in five (40 per cent) of households who call about a home emergency do so because of problems with their main central heating system.

A third of households (34 per cent) claim for plumbing and drainage problems, making this the second most common home emergency, followed by home security (10 per cent).

It is possible to buy insurance to cover common repairs including roof damage, plumbing and drainage, the main heating system, the domestic power supply, the toilet unit and home security or lost keys from around £3 per month. The insurance will pay for call-out charges and up to two hours' labour costs. These policies are add-ons to your household insurance.

14 Repairs, renovations and home improvements

Even if you are moving into a brand new home, you will find that there is a certain amount of work to be done. This may only involve putting up shelves, curtains and light fittings, but you will still find that the costs quickly mount up.

Remember, your home is your home – not just an investment. In many cases you may find that the costs of repairs and renovations are not recouped on sale, but you are still prepared to pay for them as they will enhance your enjoyment of the property.

But you should also be aware that in some cases your 'improvements' can actually reduce the value of your property. So before you start using your electric drill or employing a builder to knock down a wall or remove a fireplace, bear in mind the points discussed in the following sections.

Home improvements that add value to your home

Once you have moved into your first home, you will be tempted to try and turn it into a palace. Aside from the cost of home improvement, you could find that you lose out in other ways. Mock tudor beams in your modern flat may be your idea of great design, but you are likely to find that they reduce the potential value of your home when you come to sell. As a first-time buyer you are likely to move on within three to five years, so you should ask yourself:

▌ Is it worth spending all this money on improvements, when I am going to move in a few years?

▌ Will the £10,000 kitchen I am buying add £10,000 to the value of the property?

▌ Are the decorations/improvements I am planning likely to appeal to buyers when I come to sell my home or will they put buyers off?

Most expensive home improvements do not add a corresponding value to your property, but they can add 'saleability' by improving your chances of getting a quick sale at or near the asking price.

You should concentrate on the kitchen and bathroom and keeping the property in good decorative order – simple and tasteful. These are the things to bear in mind:

▌ A good quality kitchen is important. But it does not have to be expensive. You can make the most of your existing kitchen by changing the cupboard doors and worktops or by retiling.

▌ If you need extra space a loft conversion is an option. However, £10,000 spent will generally add only £4,000 to the value of the property. Also be aware that it will affect the appearance of the property, and if it is not in keeping with others in the street, could adversely affect its value.

▌ A separate toilet (even if it is tucked away under the stairs and it doubles as a cloakroom) adds value and can be relatively inexpensive. But don't compromise on valuable living or bedroom space.

▌ Don't get rid of original features such as cornicing, wood panelling or fireplaces, and if they have been removed consider replacing them with originals from a reclamation yard. A period property with original or sympathetically restored features can often achieve 5 to 15 per cent more than properties with none of these features. Double glazing rarely recoups its cost on sale and on period properties properly restored sash windows are more appealing to buyers than modern aluminium ones.

■ Extensions usually require planning permission and should be in sympathy with the style of your property. And conservatories, while adding extra room, may also add less value than the cost of building one. Be aware of compromising garden space.

■ Often cheaper improvements add more value – a new front door or better lighting.

■ A power shower (rather than expensive instalments such as a jacuzzi) will add value and save on your hot water bills.

■ Don't knock down walls unless you have to. It can reduce the value of your home (fewer rooms generally mean a lower price) unless you have plenty of space. If you want to give the illusion of more room, an arch with sliding or double doors may be a better option.

■ Wood flooring is popular and can be inexpensive if you have existing floorboards. You can strip, sand and varnish the floorboards yourself and should find this cheaper than having wall-to-wall carpets fitted.

■ Taste is very subjective. Avocado bathroom suites and swirly brown carpets may come back into vogue, but it is better to stick to white in the bathroom and plain carpets if you want to ensure the maximum value of your property when you come to sell.

Improvements that add the most value

Building a garage or an off-road parking bay is now the top investment to increase your property's worth, according to a survey by The One account. And with recent research showing car parking is the biggest cause of rows between neighbours, a garage is also the key to a harmonious home. A garage costs between £15,000 and £40,000 to erect but the outlay is likely to be recouped in full – and perhaps even more in London.

According to the valuation experts at The One account, the adding value improvements from worst to best are:

▌ Garden makeover costs £3,000 to £6,000 and recoups just 10 per cent of the cost.

▌ Double glazing costs £4,000 to £15,000 and recoups 25 per cent.

▌ Central heating costs £3,000 to £6,000 and recoups 25 per cent.

▌ Conservatory costs £5,000 to £25,000 and recoups 40 per cent.

▌ Electrical wiring costs £2,000 to £4,000 and recoups 50 per cent.

▌ Under-floor heating costs £2,000 to £4,000 and recoups 50 per cent.

▌ Kitchen refit costs £2,000 and recoups 50 per cent.

▌ Rear or side extension costs £7,000 to £20,000 and recoups 60 per cent.

▌ New bathroom costs £7,000 to £20,000 and recoups 75 per cent plus.

▌ Loft conversion costs £15,000 to £30,000 and recoups 75 per cent plus.

▌ Garages/off-street parking bays cost £15,000 to £40,000 but can recoup 100 per cent plus.

And some home improvements turn off potential buyers, including external rendering or cladding, a swimming pool, paving over the front garden, PVC fascias, timber-effect laminated flooring and fitted bedroom furniture.

Major works

If you need to start major building work, always contact your local council planning department for permission. In a conservation area there are likely to be restrictions on any work that will affect the appearance and character of the property. All new building work must conform to building regulations. Council building-control officers are entitled to inspect work and charge a fee for approving it.

If you live in a terraced or semi-detached house and undertake work that affects the party wall you normally need written agreement from your neighbours.

Building work almost always costs far more than you expect. So before starting work bear in mind the following:

■ Obtain realistic quotes – don't always go for the cheapest if that means cutting corners, the quote could be increased halfway through work or, because the work becomes uneconomic for the builder, he takes on other work and yours takes far longer than expected.

■ Get fixed prices if possible and do not agree hourly or daily rates as these are incentives for the builder to spend longer on the job.

■ Consider employing an architect if you want an extension or major work. A chartered surveyor can be employed for smaller alterations.

For advice on choosing an architect contact the advisory services of:

The Royal Institute of British Architects: 020 7307 3700
Royal Incorporation of Architects in Scotland: 0131 229 7205
Royal Institute of the Architects of Ireland: 00 3531 676 1703

For advice on choosing a surveyor contact the advisory services of:

The Royal Institution of Chartered Surveyors: 020 7222 7000
The Royal Institution of Chartered Surveyors in Scotland:
0131 225 7078

Do not change your mind once you have agreed on what work will
be done. Any changes to the contract or extra works are normally
charged at a higher rate. Allow for contingencies such as the
discovery of damp or woodrot.

Employing a builder

We have all heard horror stories about builders taking three times
as long as expected to complete work, charging five times as much
as agreed or disappearing halfway through a job. Employing a
builder is bound to be stressful – even if you pick a good one. You
will have workmen in your home, they will create dust and you
will get fed up with the fact that they keep drinking your tea or
arrive while you are still in bed.

To minimize the stress follow these tips:

▌ Where possible, employ a builder/electrician/handyman who
has been recommended to you – ask your neighbours, the
estate agent, etc.

▌ Pick a builder/electrician/workman who is a member of a trade
body such as The Federation of Master Builders which keeps
the National Register of Warranted Builders (builders are
bound by a code of practice and offer a warranty covering work
in progress and any defects arising from faulty workmanship
or materials within the first two years and any structural
damage for a further eight years). The telephone numbers for
these are 020 7242 7583 and 020 7404 4155 respectively.

▌ Get estimates from two or three builders and make sure you
ask them to quote for exactly the same work by typing out a
specification list.

- Make sure that any contracts you sign are specific and write in any additional clauses you think are necessary.

- Be wary of paying money in advance. Stage payments – with a small amount up-front and then payments as each stage of the work is completed – will protect you should the builder run off with your money and give an incentive for the builder to complete work quickly.

- Think twice about paying cash in hand so the builder can avoid VAT and tax. Not only will this mean you do not get a guarantee or warranty, but you may find it difficult to pursue your case in the courts if the building work is shoddy – or worse, half your home is demolished because you have employed a cowboy.

Employing an electrician

Contact the National Inspection Council for Electrical Installation Contracting for a list of approved electrical contractors and information about electricity in the home (020 7564 2323 or www.niceic.org.uk) or the Electrical Contractors Association for lists of members (020 7313 4800 or visit www.eca.co.uk).

Employing a plumber

The Institute of Plumbing has a register of plumbers which is monitored by the British Standards Institution (01708 472791).

Do-it-yourself

As a first-time buyer you may not have enough cash to pay for someone else to do work for you. Only undertake jobs that mean you will make savings. In some cases it can be cheaper to employ a professional who can not only complete the work to a higher standard and more quickly, but can buy materials at trade prices. Before starting:

▌ Make sure you can complete the work and will not have to pay a builder to complete it for you – or worse to repair any damage you have done.

▌ Buy materials at wholesalers or trade outlets if possible. You will find the costs are much lower.

▌ Don't tackle anything for which you are not qualified, especially anything to do with electricity or gas (only qualified gas fitters are allowed to connect a gas supply to an appliance).

▌ To cut costs and make work easier, consider hiring the equipment professionals use.

15 Once you have moved in

Reducing your household bills

It is only when you become a property owner, that you realize how much running a home actually costs. The cost of owning and running a home is rising well above inflation (it was up by 7.2 per cent during 2001/2002 compared to inflation of 2.7 per cent) and there are more increases in the pipeline as mortgage rates rise.

Council tax bills have already seen significant increases with this alone accounting for an average of 14 per cent of the costs of owning and running a home, with an average tax of £967 (in 2002/2003) for a Band D home in England. Increases are also expected in water, gas and electricity bills. One forecast predicts that the average annual rise in water bills will be 2.5 per cent in real terms over the next five years.

Mortgage interest payments, council tax and water rates account for about half the total cost, with maintenance (8 per cent), water supply (5 per cent), power (12 per cent), household insurance (5 per cent), telephone accounts (8 per cent) and other goods and services, appliances and tools making up the remainder.

There are regional variations in annual home running costs:

London	£7,524.43
South East	£6,487.76
East	£5,592.05
South West	£5,293.94
North West	£5,167.10

East Midlands	£5,065.51
West Midlands	£5,010.66
Yorkshire & Humberside	£4,910.09
North East	£4,900.90
AVERAGE	£5,689.63

Source: Office of National Statistics Family Spending Survey 2001/2002

To keep your bills to the minimum consider the following.

Council tax

One of the few times that you can challenge your council tax valuation is after you move into a property. But be careful that the valuations tribunal does not put your home into a higher council tax band.

Water metering

It usually pays to have a water meter installed only if you have a high rateable value and low consumption.

Gas

The deregulation of the gas market means that some 19 million consumers can shop around for the cheapest deal. You will still have the same gas supplied via the existing pipes and meter. The only difference is who sells you the gas and sends the bill. Watch out for the small print if you plan to switch companies. You will have to sign a binding contract. Prices will depend on how much gas you use and how you pay, with a discount for those who pay by direct debit. Compare the standing charge as well as the price per unit. Some suppliers offer incentives such as cashbacks, price discounts or money-off vouchers. If you sign a fixed contract you will normally have to pay a fee if you want to cancel the contract early.

The average gas bill can be cut by 10 per cent or more by shopping around. The savings on a three-bedroom house can be as much as £100.

Telephone

You will probably spend between £200 and £300 a year on your telephone bill – if not more. Although it may not seem worthwhile switching phone services to save £50 or so a year, over the long run savings do mount up.

In some cases you will be better off using an alternative to BT. The annual rental of a BT phone is over £100 – almost double the cheapest line rental from a cable company.

It is easier than ever to compare the best deals. Visit the Ofcom (the telephone watchdog Web site) at www.ofcom.org.uk or comparison sites such as www.uSwitch.com. You can save up to 90 per cent on phone calls by searching for the best deals and the service is free. You can also do a search using 'telephone bills + UK' on an Internet search engine to find other companies offering to find you the cheapest deal.

If you use your telephone for Internet connections consider broadband for greater savings. Your local cable television supplier may also be able to provide a telephone service giving you substantial savings.

Make the most of any discount schemes such as BT Friends and Family. Also, if you pay by direct debit, you could receive a discount or rebate.

If you make international calls consider using a telephone service that offers calls at much cheaper rates. You often only need to dial in a four-digit code to be connected to the cheap-rate service and do not need to change your existing telephone supplier. However, you must open an account with the company first.

Electricity/fuel bills

There are several ways in which you can cut your gas and electricity bills:

1 Install low-energy, long-life lightbulbs. They may be more expensive to buy, but over a year you can save up to £10 per bulb, or up to £60 in the bulb's lifetime of up to five years.

2 Draught proof windows and doors (you can do-it-yourself) to save up to £20 a year. Lining curtains with a thermal material and keeping them drawn as much as possible will also conserve heat.

3 Lag your hot water tank, if it is not already lagged, or buy an additional one so the jacket is at least 80 mm thick. The savings are up to £10 a year.

4 Make the most of thermostatic radiator valves to regulate the temperature of radiators – the flow of hot water is reduced once the thermostat reaches a set temperature.

5 If you live in a house, adequate loft insulation of at least 150 mm is recommended, but remember to lag pipes in the roof space to stop them freezing and to insulate your water tank.

6 Turn down your central heating thermostat by 1 degree – there will be very little difference in temperature – and savings can be up to 10 per cent.

7 Don't leave electrical items switched on or on standby unless you need to. A TV can use up to one-third as much power when it's on standby as when it's actually on.

8 If you live in a house built after 1930 and don't already have cavity wall insulation it should be considered. It can be expensive (around £600), but the savings can be up to a quarter of the price each year.

9 If you have your hot water and central heating on timer switches make sure these are used effectively and do not heat up the house or water when not necessary.

10 If you have a fireplace that you don't use, consider blocking it up (don't forget the air brick for adequate ventilation).

For further information contact your local electricity company. Most have energy efficiency teams that give free advice on energy saving.

Also visit www.uSwitch.com – you can save up to £170 a year by switching gas and electricity suppliers. If you do not have access to the Internet call 0845 601 2856.

Insurance

As discussed earlier, it pays to shop around for insurance. Remember that just because a company is the cheapest this year, it may not be next year.

Mortgage

If, after moving into your new home, you find that you could have taken out a much cheaper mortgage with another lender you can switch your home loan. But remember:

■ Some cheap mortgages are only offered to first-time buyers and you are no longer a first-time buyer.

■ If you have taken out a low-start, discount, fixed-rate or capped mortgage you may have to pay redemption penalties of several thousand pounds if you switch your mortgage in the first one to five years.

■ If you take out another mortgage you may be required to switch your endowment policy and, as such, could lose all of the premiums you have already paid.

■ Even if you have to pay redemption penalties you may still be better off switching your mortgage if the savings outweigh the additional costs.

Direct debits

If you pay your electricity, telephone and other bills by direct debit you will usually qualify for lower payments.

Dealing with leaseholder problems

If you have bought a leasehold flat or house, you may find that the freeholder fails to maintain the property properly or that you want to extend your lease or to buy the freehold.

Problems with the freeholder/management company

If you have a complaint about service charges, insurance, the cost or quality of any building works or the quality of the management of the block/building you can now take your case to a Leasehold Valuation Tribunal. These can settle disputes and, as a last resort, can appoint new managers to run blocks of flats. The role of these tribunals was strengthened under the Commonhold and Leasehold Reform Act 2002 to make them more effective and efficient. The right to seek the appointment of a new manager by the LVT was strengthened and leaseholders now have more rights against unreasonable charges levied under their lease and have greater rights to be consulted about service charges. Charges levied by landlords under Estate Management Schemes can now be challenged before a LVT and the accounting rules for leaseholders' monies have been strengthened. Landlords must also now hold service charge funds in designated separate client accounts.

Leaseholders can apply for a determination of reasonableness of charges for services, repairs, maintenance, insurance or management – including costs that have already been incurred. If there are severe problems with the management of their building they can then apply to the LVT for the removal of the manager and the appointment of a new one.

Leaseholders also now have more rights to take over the management of their property – provided certain criteria are met – and no longer need to prove fault on the part of the landlord or pay him or her any compensation.

To prevent minorities from taking control of the management of buildings at least half the flats must be on leases, with two-thirds of the flats on long leases and three-quarters of the building must be residential.

Leaseholders who exercise the right to manage will need to incorporate a company limited by guarantee.

As with any dispute, you should make sure you put all your complaints in writing and keep copies of all correspondence. Make sure you have the support of fellow leaseholders, as this will strengthen your case.

Buying the freehold/extending the lease

Under the Leasehold Reform, Housing and Urban Development Act 1993 you may be able to buy the freehold of your property or join together with others in your block of flats to purchase the freehold. The Commonhold and Leasehold Reform Act 2002 made this easier.

To acquire a new 90-year lease you must:

■ own a long lease – one which was originally for over 21 years;

■ have owned the lease for at least two years;

■ not have sublet the flat on a long lease.

Following the changes made by the Commonhold and Leasehold Reform Act 2002 the price payable is:

■ the reduction in the value of the landlord's interests in the flat as a result of the granting of the new, longer lease plus half *of any marriage value* (marriage value will only be payable on leases with less than 80 years left to run and is the extra value added to the property as a result of the longer lease); and

■ compensation (where relevant) for severance or other losses resulting from the granting of a new, longer lease (for example, loss of development value).

Further information

The Office of the Deputy Prime Minister – www.odpm.gov.uk – has several useful publications. Search under *Housing* and then *Guidance for Homeowners, Tenants and Landlords* and look under *Publications* for *Booklets for homeowners on long leaseholds.* These include:

■ *Your right to buy the freehold of your building or renew your lease.*

■ *Applying to a Leasehold Valuation Tribunal.*

■ *Lease running out? Security of tenure for long leaseholders.*

You can also contact LEASE, the Leasehold Advisory Service, at www.lease-advice.org.uk or call 0845 345 1993. LEASE produces detailed publications on buying the freehold, lease extensions, service charges and the right to manage.

For collective enfranchisement (when flat owners club together to purchase the freehold):

▌ the property must have two or more flats held by qualifying tenants;

▌ if the building was not purpose built as flats and has less than five flats it must not have a resident landlord;

▌ it must be in a single freehold ownership;

▌ the property must not include more than 25 per cent of non-residential floor space;

▌ at least two-thirds of the flats must be held by qualifying tenants with leases originally granted for at least 21 years.

Remember, if you are buying a flat with the aim of buying the freehold you will have to be a resident for at least a year (but often three years), you will have to ensure that other lessees are equally determined and you will find the procedures complex and costly (including paying both sides' fees).

The other option is where the landlord intends to sell the freehold. In this case, tenants must be given right of first refusal to buy at that price. In this case the landlord's costs do not have to be met and there are fewer restrictions on the tenants who qualify.

However, you may be able to improve the value of your flat by opting for the simpler route of a 90-year lease extension. For a start this can be done independently of other lessees. However, if you and other lessees are unhappy with the management of the building you may still want to opt for the more difficult and costly alternative of buying the freehold.

Problems paying the mortgage

As discussed in the chapter on mortgages, homebuyers are now advised to take out mortgage protection insurance to cover their mortgage repayments should they be unable to work due to ill health or redundancy.

Insurance currently costs around £5 for every £100 of monthly repayment covered and is worth buying because:

■ renters who lose their jobs can often get housing benefit if their partner is still in work, but homebuyers must struggle on one salary as they receive no benefit if one partner is working;

■ new buyers (those who bought since October 1995) get no state help with their mortgage for the first nine months if they lose their job and claim state benefits (renters get help to pay their rent almost immediately).

As you are unlikely to get state help to pay your mortgage, and if you have no insurance, you will find that you quickly fall into arrears and risk repossession. To minimize the risks:

■ Contact your mortgage lender as soon as you lose your job/find it difficult to meet your monthly mortgage repayments.

■ Ask if you can reduce or defer mortgage payments until you find a new job/sort out your finances. Lenders will normally only agree to this if you have sufficient equity in your property. If your mortgage is worth almost as much as the value of your property the lender may feel that there is a risk that, if you sell your home or it is repossessed, the sale proceeds may not cover the outstanding mortgage debt.

■ Contact your local Citizens Advice Bureau for advice on dealing with creditors.

■ Keep your mortgage lender informed of any changes in your circumstances and your attempts to find another job.

▌ Find out if you can rent the property for more than your monthly mortgage bills and ask your lender if it will agree to you renting out the property to cover the costs.

▌ Try to pay at least some of the mortgage repayments – even if you have to take a temporary job and rent out a room to do so.

▌ Avoid repossession at all costs. It will be better for you to sell the property than for it to be repossessed because:
  – if you sell the property yourself you are likely to receive a higher sale price than would be achieved if the property were sold after repossession (when it may have been left empty for several months)
  – if you sell the property yourself you will not be credit blacklisted – if it is repossessed you will find it difficult to take out another mortgage at a future date

Your mortgage lender will have to agree to the sale so discuss your plans before putting the property on the market. If you are in negative equity – the value of your property is less than your outstanding mortgage debt – you will have to prove you can repay the balance in order to get the agreement of your lender to sell the property.

▌ If you are taken to court for non-payment of your mortgage always attend the hearing and fight your case. You may be able to delay repossession for long enough to find another job.

The Council of Mortgage Lenders produces several useful publications on protecting your mortgage payments including _State help for homebuyers_ and _Take cover for a rainy day_. It also produces a range of leaflets on arrears and repossession. Visit www.cml.org.uk and look under consumer information.

Wills

Now that you are a homeowner it is important for you to draw up a will or amend your existing one. This is particularly important if you have jointly purchased the property (see joint ownership on page 71).

Two-thirds of people die without making a valid will, and yet the implications of failing to do so can be devastating. Your estranged parents, or brothers and sisters you never speak to, can receive all your estate or, worse, the person with whom you are cohabiting may not inherit the property, even though this is what you intend.

The rules of intestacy (if you fail to make a will) specify that your inheritance is split between your surviving spouse and children – if you are unmarried and childless, other relatives then inherit your estate. The rules vary depending on whether you come under English, Scottish or Northern Irish rules.

Drawing up a will

Even if you seek professional advice in drawing up a will you must make sure that it is drawn up correctly and meets your wishes. A recent *Which?* survey found that 15 out of 51 wills were poorly drawn up, and in some cases those designed to inherit may have been unable to because of confusing wording. And make sure your will covers all eventualities. For instance, if you leave a certain possession to a friend, what happens if he or she dies before you? The problem is that you will not know if your will is inadequate until it is too late.

Be wary of appointing a professional executor at the time of will writing as some of the banks can charge high fees for dealing with your will, and these can substantially reduce the value of your estate.

You can either approach a solicitor, bank, building society or life insurance company or a specialist will writing company. Will writers are members of one of the following trade bodies: the Society of Will Writers, the Willwriters Association and the Institute of Professional Willwriters. They do regulate their members, but do not have compensation schemes.

If the will is not drawn up properly it could be invalid and the rules of intestacy could apply. So if the will does not specify what happens if the main beneficiary dies before you, the will could be invalid.

Once you have drawn up a will you should review it regularly so it reflects any changes in your circumstances.

You will also need to appoint one or two executors (these can be friends or family) to administer your will on behalf of the beneficiaries.

Finally, store your will in a safe place – preferably with a third party – where it can be easily found by your executors.

Appendix: monthly mortgage costs

To calculate the monthly cost of your mortgage select the interest rate and the number of years over which you intend to borrow. Multiply the figure in the corresponding column by the number of thousands you wish to borrow. For example, borrowing £60,000 over 25 years at 4.5 per cent will cost £5.62 x 60 = £337.20 a month. Source: Council of Mortgage Lenders. For more detailed charts visit www.cml.org.uk.

Years	3.00%	3.50%	3.75%	4.00%	4.25%	4.50%	4.75%
5	18.20	18.46	18.59	18.72	18.85	18.98	19.12
10	9.77	10.02	10.15	10.27	10.40	10.53	10.66
15	6.98	7.24	7.36	7.50	7.63	7.76	7.89
16	6.63	6.89	7.02	7.15	7.28	7.42	7.55
17	6.33	6.59	6.72	6.85	6.98	7.12	7.25
18	6.06	6.32	6.45	6.58	6.72	6.85	6.99
19	5.82	6.08	6.21	6.34	6.48	6.62	6.76
20	5.60	5.86	6.00	6.13	6.27	6.41	6.55
21	5.41	5.67	5.80	5.94	6.08	6.22	6.36
22	5.23	5.49	5.63	5.77	5.91	6.05	6.19
23	5.07	5.33	5.47	5.61	5.75	5.89	6.03
24	4.92	5.19	5.33	5.47	5.61	5.75	5.89
25	4.79	5.06	5.19	5.33	5.48	5.62	5.77

26	4.66	4.93	5.07	5.21	5.36	5.50	5.65
27	4.55	4.82	4.96	5.10	5.25	5.39	5.54
28	4.44	4.72	4.86	5.00	5.15	5.29	5.44
29	4.34	4.62	4.76	4.91	5.05	5.20	5.35
30	4.25	4.53	4.67	4.82	4.97	5.12	5.27

Years	5.00%	5.25%	5.50%	5.75%	6.00%	6.25%	6.50%
5	19.25	19.38	19.51	19.65	19.78	19.92	20.05
10	10.79	10.92	11.06	11.19	11.32	11.46	11.59
15	8.03	8.16	8.30	8.44	8.58	8.72	8.86
16	7.69	7.83	7.97	8.11	8.25	8.39	8.53
17	7.39	7.53	7.67	7.81	7.95	8.10	8.24
18	7.13	7.27	7.41	7.55	7.70	7.84	7.99
19	6.90	7.04	7.18	7.32	7.47	7.62	7.76
20	6.69	6.83	6.97	7.12	7.27	7.41	7.56

Years	5.00%	5.25%	5.50%	5.75%	6.00%	6.25%	6.50%
21	6.50	6.64	6.79	6.94	7.08	7.23	7.38
22	6.33	6.48	6.62	6.77	6.92	7.07	7.22
23	6.18	6.32	6.47	6.62	6.77	6.93	7.08
24	6.04	6.19	6.34	6.49	6.64	6.79	6.95
25	5.91	6.06	6.21	6.36	6.52	6.67	6.83
26	5.80	5.95	6.10	6.25	6.41	6.57	6.72
27	5.69	5.84	6.00	6.15	6.31	6.47	6.63
28	5.59	5.75	5.90	6.06	6.22	6.38	6.54
29	5.50	5.66	5.81	5.97	6.13	6.29	6.46
30	5.42	5.58	5.73	5.89	6.05	6.22	6.38

Appendix

Years	6.75%	7.00%	7.25%	7.50%
5	20.19	20.32	20.46	20.60
10	11.73	11.86	12.00	12.14
15	9.01	9.15	9.29	9.44
16	8.68	8.82	8.97	9.12
17	8.39	8.54	8.68	8.83
18	8.14	8.28	8.43	8.59
19	7.91	8.06	8.21	8.37
20	7.71	7.87	8.02	8.17
21	7.54	7.69	7.85	8.00
22	7.38	7.53	7.69	7.85
23	7.24	7.39	7.55	7.71
24	7.11	7.27	7.43	7.59
25	6.99	7.15	7.31	7.48
26	6.88	7.05	7.21	7.37
27	6.79	6.95	7.12	7.28
28	6.70	6.87	7.03	7.20
29	6.62	6.79	6.96	7.12
30	6.55	6.72	6.88	7.06

Index

Also available from Kogan Page in *The Complete Guide to ...* series:

The Complete Guide to Buying and Selling Property
second edition, Sarah O'Grady

The Complete Guide to Buying Property Abroad
second edition, Liz Hodgkinson

The Complete Guide to Buying Property in France
second edition, Charles Davey

The Complete Guide to Buying Property in Italy
Barbara McMahon

The Complete Guide to Buying Property in Spain
Charles Davey

The Complete Guide to Letting Property
second edition, Liz Hodgkinson

The Complete Guide to Renovating and Improving Your Property
Liz Hodgkinson

The above titles are available from all good bookshops. To obtain further information, please contact the publisher at the address below:

Kogan Page
120 Pentonville Road
London N1 9JN
Tel: 020 7278 0433
Fax: 020 7837 6348
www.kogan-page.co.uk